تَسْهِيْلُ النَّحْوِ

TASHEEL AL-NAHW

ver 2.1

تَسْهِيْلُ النَّحْوِ
TASHEEL AL-NAHW
ver 2.1

based on
'Ilm al-Nahw of Mawlana Mushtaq Ahmad Charthawali

Revised by
'Aamir Bashir

Copyright © Dār al-Saʿādah Publications 2011
First Online Edition Jul 2011
Second Online Edition Jul 2012
Version 2.1 Jan 2014
Updated Dec 2014

ilmresources.wordpress.com

"General and unrestricted permission is granted for the unaltered duplication, distribution, and transmission of this text."

In Plain English: Make as many copies as you want.

TABLE OF CONTENTS

Table of Contents	i
List of Tables	vii
Acknowledgments	ix
Foreword	xi
اَلْاِصْطِلَاحَاتُ الْعَرَبِيَّةُ – Arabic Terms	xiii

CHAPTER 1 — 1

1.1. اَلنَّحْوُ – Arabic Grammar	1
1.2 اَلْكَلِمَةُ – The Word	2
اِسْمٌ – Noun	2
فِعْلٌ – Verb	3
حَرْفٌ – Particle	3
1.3	4
أَقْسَامُ الِاسْمِ – Types of Noun	4
أَقْسَامُ الْفِعْلِ – Types of Verb	4
أَقْسَامُ الْحَرْفِ – Types of Particle	4
1.4 الْجُمَلُ وَالْمُرَكَّبَاتُ – Sentences and Phrases	6
1.4.1 أَقْسَامُ الْجُمْلَةِ الْخَبَرِيَّةِ	6
جُمْلَةٌ اسْمِيَّةٌ خَبَرِيَّةٌ – Nominal Sentence	6
جُمْلَةٌ فِعْلِيَّةٌ خَبَرِيَّةٌ – Verbal Sentence	7
1.4.2 أَقْسَامُ الْجُمْلَةِ الْإِنْشَائِيَّةِ	8
1.4.3 أَقْسَامُ الْمُرَكَّبِ النَّاقِصِ – Types of Phrases	9
1. اَلْمُرَكَّبُ التَّوْصِيفِيُّ – Descriptive Phrase	9
2. اَلْمُرَكَّبُ الْإِضَافِيُّ – Possessive Phrase	9
3. اَلْمُرَكَّبُ الْإِشَارِيُّ – Demonstrative Phrase	10
4. اَلْمُرَكَّبُ الْبِنَائِيُّ/ الْعَدَدِيُّ – Numerical Phrase	10

	5. اَلْمُرَكَّبُ مَنْعُ الصَّرْفِ – Indeclinable Phrase	11
	1.4.4 Additional Notes About جُمْلَةٌ اِسْمِيَّةٌ	14
Summary		15
1.5		16
	عَلَامَاتُ الْإِسْمِ – Signs of a Noun	16
	عَلَامَاتُ الْفِعْلِ – Signs of a Verb	16
	عَلَامَةُ الْحَرْفِ – Sign of a Particle	16
	1.5.1 General Notes	17
1.6	اَلضَّمَائِرُ – Personal Pronouns	19
1.7	اَلْحُرُوفُ الْجَارَّةُ – Prepositions	20
1.8	اَلْحُرُوفُ الْمُشَبَّهَةُ بِالْفِعْلِ – Those Particles That Resemble the Verb	22
1.9	اَلْأَفْعَالُ النَّاقِصَةُ – Auxiliary (Defective) Verbs	25

CHAPTER 2   27
اَلْمُعْرَبُ وَالْمَبْنِيُّ – Declinable and Indeclinable Words

2.1		27
	عَلَامَاتُ الْإِعْرَابِ – Signs of *I'raab*	27
	حَالَاتُ الْمُعْرَبِ – Conditions of *Mu'rab*	27
	Difference Between كَسْرٌ – فَتْحٌ – ضَمٌّ and كَسْرَةٌ – فَتْحَةٌ – ضَمَّةٌ	28
2.2	اَلْمَبْنِيُّ – Indeclinable Word	29
	اَلْإِعْرَابُ الْمَحَلِّيْ	30
2.3	اَلْمُعْرَبُ – Declinable Word	31
2.4	أَقْسَامُ الْأَسْمَاءِ الْمَبْنِيَّةِ – Types of Indeclinable Nouns	32
	2.4.1 اَلضَّمَائِرُ – Personal Pronouns	33
	2.4.2 اَلْأَسْمَاءُ الْمَوصُولَةُ - Relative Pronouns	39
	2.4.3 أَسْمَاءُ الْإِشَارَةِ – Demonstrative Pronouns	42
	2.4.4 أَسْمَاءُ الْأَفْعَالِ – Those Nouns Which Have the Meaning of Verbs	45
	2.4.5 أَسْمَاءُ الْأَصْوَاتِ – Those Nouns Which Denote a Sound	46

2.4.6	اَلظُّرُوفُ – Adverbs	47
	ظُرُوفُ الزَّمَانِ – Adverbs of Time	47
	ظُرُوفُ الْمَكَانِ – Adverbs of Place	49
2.4.7	اَلْكِنَايَاتُ – Those Nouns Which Indicate an Unspecified Quantity	52
2.4.8	اَلْمُرَكَّبُ الْبِنَائِيُّ – Numerical phrase	52
2.5	أَقْسَامُ الْأَسْمَاءِ الْمُعْرَبَةِ – Types of Declinable Nouns	53
	مُنْصَرِفٌ	53
	غَيْرُ مُنْصَرِفٍ	53
	أَسْبَابُ مَنْعِ الصَّرْفِ	53
2.6	إِعْرَابُ أَقْسَامِ الْأَسْمَاءِ الْمُعْرَبَاتِ – *I'raab* of the Various Types of *Mu'rab* Nouns	58

CHAPTER 3   61
Further Discussion of Nouns

3.1	اَلْاِسْمُ الْمَنْسُوبُ – Relative Adjective	61
3.2	اَلْاِسْمُ التَّصْغِيرُ – Diminutive Noun	63
3.3	اَلْمَعْرِفَةُ وَالنَّكِرَةُ – Definite and Common Nouns	64
3.4	اَلْاِسْمُ الْمُذَكَّرُ وَالْمُؤَنَّثُ – Masculine and Feminine Nouns	65
3.5	وَاحِدٌ وَتَثْنِيَةٌ وَجَمْعٌ – Singular, Dual and Plural	67
3.6	أَقْسَامُ الْجَمْعِ – Types of Plural	68
3.7	اَلْمَرْفُوعَاتُ - Words Which Are Always *Marfoo'*	73
	3.7.1 فَاعِلٌ – Subject/Doer	73
	3.7.2 مَفْعُولٌ مَالَمْ يُسَمَّ فَاعِلُهُ / نَائِبُ الْفَاعِلِ – Substitute of فَاعِلٌ	75
	3.7.3 اِسْمُ مَا وَلَا الْمُشَبَّهَتَيْنِ بِ لَيْسَ – The Noun of Those مَا and لَا, Which Are Similar to لَيْسَ	76
	3.7.4 خَبَرُ لَا الَّتِي لِنَفْيِ الْجِنْسِ – The خَبَرٌ of That لَا Which Negates an Entire (Class) جِنْسٌ	77
3.8	اَلْمَنْصُوبَاتُ – Words Which Are Always *Mansoob*	79
	3.8.1 مَفْعُولٌ بِهِ – Object	79

3.8.2 مَفْعُولٌ مُطْلَقٌ		81
3.8.3 مَفْعُولٌ لِأَجْلِهِ / مَفْعُولٌ لَهُ		81
3.8.4 مَفْعُولٌ مَعَهُ		81
3.8.5 ظَرْفٌ / مَفْعُولٌ فِيهِ		82
3.8.6 حَالٌ – State / Condition		84
3.8.7 تَمْيِيزٌ / تَمْيِزٌ		87
Rules for أَسْمَاءُ الْعَدَدِ (Numerals)		88
3.8.8 مُسْتَثْنَى		92
3.9 اَلْمَجْرُورَاتُ – Words Which Are Always *Majroor*		95
3.10 اَلتَّوَابِعُ		96
3.10.1 اَلنَّعْتُ أَوِ الصِّفَةُ – Adjective		96
3.10.2 اَلتَّأْكِيدُ – Emphasis		100
3.10.3 اَلْبَدَلُ – Substitute		103
3.10.4 اَلْعَطْفُ بِحَرْفٍ/عَطْفُ النَّسَقِ – Conjunction		105
حُرُوفُ الْعَطْفِ		105
3.10.5 عَطْفُ الْبَيَانِ		108

CHAPTER 4 — 109

اَلْعَوَامِلُ – Governing Words

4.1 اَلْحُرُوفُ الْعَامِلَةُ – Governing Particles		110
Particles Which Govern Nouns		110
Particles Which Govern فِعْلٌ مُضَارِعٌ		110
4.1.1 اَلْحُرُوفُ النَّاصِبَةُ – Particles That Give *Nasb*		111
4.1.2 اَلْحُرُوفُ الْجَازِمَةُ – Particles That Give *Jazm*		114
4.2 اَلْأَفْعَالُ الْعَامِلَةُ – Governing Verbs		116
4.2.1 اَلْفِعْلُ الْمَعْرُوفُ – Active Verb		116
4.2.2 اَلْفِعْلُ الْمَجْهُولُ – Passive Verb		116
4.2.3 اَلْفِعْلُ اللَّازِمُ – Intransitive Verb		116

4.2.4 اَلْأَفْعَالُ النَّاقِصَةُ		116
4.2.5 اَلْفِعْلُ الْمُتَعَدِّيْ – Transitive Verb		117
4.2.6 أَفْعَالُ الْمُقَارَبَةِ وَالرَّجَاءِ وَالشُّرُوْعِ		119
4.2.7 أَفْعَالُ الْمَدْحِ وَالذَّمّ – Verbs of Praise and Blame		121
4.2.8 أَفْعَالُ التَّعَجُّبِ – Verbs of Wonder		123
4.3 اَلْأَسْمَاءُ الْعَامِلَةُ – Governing Nouns		124
4.3.1 اَلْأَسْمَاءُ الشَّرْطِيَّةُ – Conditional Nouns		124
4.3.2 اِسْمُ الْفَاعِلِ		126
4.3.2.1 اِسْمُ الْمُبَالَغَةِ		127
4.3.3 اِسْمُ الْمَفْعُوْلِ		129
4.3.4 اَلصِّفَةُ الْمُشَبَّهَةُ بِاسْمِ الْفَاعِلِ – That Adjective Which is Similar to اِسْمُ الْفَاعِلِ		130
4.3.5 اِسْمُ التَّفْضِيْلِ		132
4.3.6 اَلْمَصْدَرُ		134
4.3.7 اَلْمُضَافُ		135
4.3.8 اَلْاِسْمُ التَّامُ		135
4.3.9 اَلْكِنَايَاتُ		136
4.4 اَلْحُرُوْفُ الْغَيْرُ الْعَامِلَةِ – Non-Governing Particles		137
1. حُرُوْفُ التَّنْبِيْهِ – Particles of Notification		137
2. حُرُوْفُ الْإِيْجَابِ – Particles of Affirmation		137
3. حَرْفَا التَّفْسِيْرِ – Particles of Clarification		138
4. اَلْحُرُوْفُ الْمَصْدَرِيَّةُ		138
5. حُرُوْفُ التَّحْضِيْضِ – Particles of Exhortation		138
6. حَرْفُ التَّوَقُّعِ – Particle of Anticipation		139
7. حَرْفَا الْاِسْتِفْهَامِ – Particles of Interrogation		139
8. حَرْفُ الرَّدْعِ – Particle of Rebuke		140
9. اَلتَّنْوِيْنُ		140

10. نُوْنُ التَّأْكِيْدِ	140
11. حَرْفُ لَ	140
12. اَلْحُرُوْفُ الزَّائِدَةُ – Extra Particles	141
13. حُرُوْفُ الشَّرْطِ الَّتِيْ لَا تَجْزِمُ – Conditional Particles That Do Not Give *Jazm*	142
14. مَا (مَا دَامَ)	143
15. حُرُوْفُ الْعَطْفِ	143

Appendix   145

Bibliography   149

LIST OF TABLES

Table No		Page No
1.1	اَلضَّمَائِرُ – Personal Pronouns	19
1.2	اَلْحُرُوفُ الْجَارَّةُ – Prepositions	20
1.3	اَلْحُرُوفُ الْمُشَبَّهَةُ بِالْفِعْلِ – Those Particles That Resemble the Verb	22
1.4	اَلْأَفْعَالُ النَّاقِصَةُ – Auxiliary (Defective) Verbs	25
2.1	حَالَةُ الرَّفْعِ in (also called ضَمِيْرٌ مَرْفُوْعٌ مُنْفَصِلٌ) ضَمِيْرٌ مُنْفَصِلٌ (بَارِزٌ)	34
2.2	حَالَةُ الرَّفْعِ in (also called ضَمِيْرٌ مَرْفُوْعٌ مُتَّصِلٌ) ضَمِيْرٌ مُتَّصِلٌ	35
2.3	حَالَةُ النَّصْبِ in (also called ضَمِيْرٌ مَنْصُوْبٌ مُتَّصِلٌ and ضَمِيْرٌ مُنْفَصِلٌ) ضَمِيْرٌ مَنْصُوْبٌ مُتَّصِلٌ and مُنْفَصِلٌ	36
2.4	حَالَةُ الْجَرِّ in (also called ضَمِيْرٌ مَجْرُوْرٌ مُتَّصِلٌ) ضَمِيْرٌ مُتَّصِلٌ (بَارِزٌ)	37
2.5	اَلْأَسْمَاءُ الْمَوْصُوْلَةُ لِلْمُذَكَّرِ	39
2.6	اَلْأَسْمَاءُ الْمَوْصُوْلَةُ لِلْمُؤَنَّثِ	39
2.7	أَسْمَاءُ الْإِشَارَةِ لِلْمُذَكَّرِ	42
2.8	أَسْمَاءُ الْإِشَارَةِ لِلْمُؤَنَّثِ	42
2.9	Nouns in the Meaning of اَلْفِعْلُ الْمَاضِيْ	45
2.10	Nouns in the Meaning of اَلْأَمْرُ الْحَاضِرُ	45
2.11	إِعْرَابُ أَقْسَامِ الْأَسْمَاءِ الْمُعْرَبَاتِ	59
3.1	أَوْزَانُ جَمْعِ قِلَّةٍ	69
3.2	أَوْزَانُ جَمْعِ كَثْرَةٍ	69
3.3	أَمْثَالُ جَمْعِ الْجَمْعِ	70
3.4	أَوْزَانُ مُنْتَهَى الْجُمُوْعِ	70
3.5	اِسْتِعْمَالُ الْفِعْلِ حَسْبَ الْفَاعِلِ	73
3.6	Different Forms of the Noun of لَا and Its *I'raab*	77
3.7	Rules Governing the *I'raab* of مُنَادَى	80

3.8	إِعْرَابُ الْمُسْتَثْنَى	93
4.1	اَلْحُرُوفُ النَّاصِبَةُ	111
4.2	اَلْحُرُوفُ الْجَازِمَةُ	114
4.3	أَفْعَالُ الْقُلُوبِ	117
4.4	Verbs Requiring Three مَفْعُولٌ بِهِ	118
4.5	أَفْعَالُ الْمُقَارَبَةِ وَالرَّجَاءِ وَالشُّرُوعِ	119
4.6	اَلْأَسْمَاءُ الشَّرْطِيَّةُ	124
4.7	أَوْزَانُ اسْمِ الْمُبَالَغَةِ	127
4.8	أَوْزَانُ الصِّفَةِ الْمُشَبَّهَةِ	130
4.9	أَوْزَانُ اسْمِ التَّفْضِيلِ	132

ACKNOWLEDGMENTS

There are many people whom I would like to thank for making this project a success. To begin with, I am in debt to the sister who typed up the old *Tasheel al-Nahw*, and thus helped to kick-start the project. She does not want her name to be publicized. I would also like to thank Mawlana Ibrahim Memon and his students of Darul Uloom al-Madania's eAlim program for their valuable feedback. Last but not the least, I am indebted to my First year students at Darul Uloom al-Madania (both 2010–2011 and 2011–2012), who have been continuously giving me feedback. I would especially like to mention my current First year students 'Abdullah, Ayyub, Muhammad, Sa'eed, Umair, Umar, and Wahid. I have greatly benefitted from their intelligent questions, wise comments, useful suggestions, and help with proof-reading. May Allah reward them, and all others for their contributions and help.

بسم الله الرحمن الرحيم
نحمده و نصلي على رسوله الكريم

FOREWORD

This book is the second edition of the revised *Tasheel al-Nahw*, which in turn was a somewhat expanded translation of the Urdu language primer of Arabic grammar, *'Ilm al-Nahw* by Mawlana Mushtaq Ahmad Charthawali. Mawlana Charthawali's primers for *Nahw* (Arabic grammar) and *Sarf* (Arabic Morphology) are standard textbooks in Western *madrasahs*. The original English translation of *'Ilm al-Nahw* was prepared by scholars from Madrasah Islamiyyah, Benoni, South Africa. They put in a lot of hardwork and made the English translation much more beneficial than the Urdu original. May Allah reward them. At least two versions of this translation are available online. The first one had many errors and typing issues. The newer version made some improvements but issues remained, especially with regards to language and clarity of the English and Arabic texts. In 2010, we decided to bring out a revised edition of this translation to address these issues. During the course of our revision and editing, we consulted various grammar works including *al-Nahw al-Wadih*, *Sharh ibn 'Aqil*, *Mu'jam al-Qawa'id al-'Arabiyyah*, and *A Simplified Arabic Grammar*. We completely revised some sections, as well as a number of definitions. The organization was changed in a way that we felt would make it easier for students to understand how each section fits in the overall picture.

This second edition has undergone more changes. Further improvements have been made in many sections; some sections have been completely revised; confusing sentences have been elaborated; more examples and exercises have been included, including many from *al-Nahw al-Wadih* and *Mu'allim al-Insha'*; and where needed, the relevant *al-Nahw al-Wadih* section has been pointed out in the footnotes. These footnotes are for the benefit of the teachers. The students can choose to ignore them. Lastly, an appendix has been attached at the end, identifying *Tasheel al-Nahw*'s place in *Nahw* texts, as well as suggesting a possible curriculum of classical Arabic studies.

This is a beginner-to-intermediate level text; therefore, we have not transliterated Arabic words exactly, keeping in mind that most people at this stage will not be comfortable with Arabic transliteration schemes. Rather, we have used approximate equivalents that are easier to read for the untrained. Nevertheless, non-English words have been italicized to reflect their non-English origin. The documentation in the foot-notes does not follow any particular academic standard; rather, it has been modified for ease of the students. It should also be noted that the English equivalents of Arabic grammar terms are mere approximations. In some cases, they convey the exact meaning. In many cases, they do not. The student is, therefore, urged to focus on the original term in Arabic.

We would also like to point out that this is not a do-it-yourself text. First of all, it assumes some prior knowledge of Arabic such as that acquired through studying *Ten Lessons of Arabic* and/or *Durus al-Lughah al-'Arabiyyah* vol. 1. Moreover, it needs to be studied with a teacher. However, it can be used as a revision text by those who have already studied *Nahw* using other texts. It is respectfully suggested to the teachers to also use *al-Nahw al-Wadih* (all six volumes) while teaching, as reference and for additional examples and exercises, as and when needed. Moreover, it should also be pointed out that this is not an exhaustive text. It does not cover every issue of *Nahw*, in brief or in detail. It is assumed that the student will be studying relatively advanced *Nahw* texts (such as *Hidayat al-Nahw* or *al-Nahw al-Wadih*) after this to round off his/her training of *Nahw*. The sample curriculum given in the appendix can be used for that purpose.

To the best of our ability, we have tried to remove all errors. However, we are merely human. There are bound to be some mistakes in it, and definitely, room for improvement. Your comments, constructive criticism, and suggestions are all welcome. You can contact us with your feedback at the email address given at the end.

We hope and pray that this revised translation will be of benefit to the students. We also pray that Allah Most High accepts this humble effort from all those who have contributed to it in any way, and gives us the power to continue with more. We also request the readers and all those who benefit from it in any way to remember us in their prayers.

And He alone gives success.

وَصَلَّى اللهُ تَعَالَى عَلَى خَيْرِ خَلْقِهِ سَيِّدِنَا وَمَوْلَانَا مُحَمَّدٍ وَّعَلَى اٰلِهِ وَأَصْحَابِهِ أَجْمَعِيْنَ

'Aamir Bashir
Buffalo, NY
14th Sha'ban, 1433 (4th July, 2012)
E-mail: ainbay97@gmail.com

الْاِصْطِلَاحَاتُ الْعَرَبِيَّةُ

ARABIC TERMS

Arabic Term	Approximate Transliteration	Equivalent English Term / Description of the meaning
اِسْمٌ	ism	Noun
فِعْلٌ	fi'l	Verb
حَرْفٌ	harf	Particle
مُذَكَّرٌ	mudhakkar	Masculine
مُؤَنَّثٌ	mu'annath	Feminine
وَاحِدٌ	waahid	Singular
تَثْنِيَةٌ	tathniyah	Dual
جَمْعٌ	jam'	Plural
ضَمَّةٌ	dammah	ُ
فَتْحَةٌ	fathah	َ
كَسْرَةٌ	kasrah	ِ
حَرَكَةٌ جَمْعٌ: حَرَكَاتٌ	harakah plural: harakaat	Short vowels, i.e., *dammah* ُ, *fathah* َ, *kasrah* ِ
حُرُوفُ الْعِلَّةِ	huroof al-'illah	Long vowels i.e., و – ا – ي
إِعْرَابٌ	i'raab	These are the variations at the end of the word, which take place in accordance with the governing word.
تَنْوِيْنٌ	tanween	two *fathahs* (ً), two *dammahs* (ٌ), two *kasrahs* (ٍ)
سُكُوْنٌ	sukoon	ْ
سَاكِنٌ	saakin	A letter with *sukoon*
تَشْدِيْدٌ	tashdeed	ّ
مُشَدَّدٌ	mushaddad	A letter with *tashdeed*
فَاعِلٌ	faa'il	Subject i.e. the doer
مَفْعُوْلٌ	maf'ool	Object i.e. the person or thing upon whom or which the work is done.
عَامِلٌ	'aamil	Governing word i.e. that word, which causes *i'raab* change in the word(s) following it.

Arabic Term	Approximate Transliteration	Equivalent English Term / Description of the meaning
مَعْمُوْلٌ	ma'mool	The governed word i.e. that word in which the *i'raab* change occurred.
فِعْلٌ مَعْرُوْفٌ	fi'l ma'roof	The active verb i.e. that verb whose doer is known/mentioned.
فِعْلٌ مَجْهُوْلٌ	fi'l majhool	The passive verb i.e. that verb whose doer is not known/mentioned.
فِعْلٌ لَازِمٌ	fi'l laazim	The intransitive verb i.e. that verb, which can be understood without a مَفْعُوْلٌ.
اَلْفِعْلُ الْمُتَعَدِّيْ	fi'l muta'addi	The transitive verb i.e. that verb, which cannot be fully understood without a مَفْعُوْلٌ.
مَعْرِفَةٌ	ma'rifah	Definite noun. It is generally indicated by an ال. For example, اَلْبَيْتُ <u>the</u> house (a particular/specific house).
نَكِرَةٌ	nakirah	Common noun. It is generally indicated by a *tanween*. e.g. بَيْتٌ <u>a</u> house (any house).
مَرْفُوْعٌ	marfoo'	It is that word, which is in the state of رَفْعٌ, which is generally represented by a *dammah* on the last letter.
مَنْصُوْبٌ	mansoob	It is that word, which is in the state of نَصْبٌ, which is generally represented by a *fathah* on the last letter.
مَجْرُوْرٌ	majroor	It is that word, which is in the state of جَرٌّ, which is generally represented by a *kasrah* on the last letter.

CHAPTER 1

Section 1.1
اَلنَّحْوُ – Arabic Grammar

Definition:
Nahw is that science, which teaches us how to join a noun, verb and particle to form a correct sentence, as well as what the إِعْرَابٌ (condition) of the last letter of a word should be.

Subject Matter:
Its subject matter is كَلِمَةٌ (word) and كَلَامٌ (sentence).

Objective:
- The immediate objective is to learn how to read, write and speak Arabic correctly, and to avoid making mistakes in this. For example, زَيْد, دَار, دَخَلَ, and فِي are four words. The science of *Nahw* teaches us how to put them together to form a correct sentence.
- The mid-term objective is to use our Arabic skills to understand the *Qur'an*, *Hadeeth*, *Fiqh* and other Islamic sciences, so that we can act upon them.
- The ultimate objective through the above is to gain the pleasure of Allah Most High.

Section 1.2
اَلْكَلِمَةُ – The Word

Any word uttered by humans is called a لَفْظٌ. If it has a meaning, it is called مَوْضُوْعٌ (meaningful); and if it does not have any meaning, it is called مُهْمَلٌ (meaningless).

In Arabic, لَفْظٌ مَوْضُوْعٌ (meaningful word) is of two types: مُفْرَدٌ and مُرَكَّبٌ.

1. مُفْرَدٌ – Singular: It is that single word, which conveys one meaning. It is also called كَلِمَةٌ.
2. مُرَكَّبٌ – Compound: It is a group of words. They may form a complete sentence or an incomplete one.

Types of كَلِمَةٌ

There are three types of كَلِمَةٌ:

1. اِسْمٌ (noun)
2. فِعْلٌ (verb)
3. حَرْفٌ (particle)

اِسْمٌ – Noun:

- It is that كَلِمَةٌ whose meaning can be understood without the need to combine it with another word.
- It does not have any tense.[1]
- It is the name of a person, place or thing.[2]

    e.g.   رَجُلٌ   man
           اَلْبَيْتُ   house

Note: A noun can never have a تَنْوِيْنٌ (*tanween*) and an ال at the same time.

---

[1] The first two bullets combine to form the classical definition of اِسْمٌ. See, for example, 'Abdullah ibn 'Aqil, *Sharh ibn 'Aqil 'ala Alfiyyat ibn Malik*, (Cairo: Dar al-Turath, 1980), vol. 1, 15. The definition given by ibn 'Aqil is as follows: (اَلْكَلِمَةُ إِنْ دَلَّتْ عَلَى مَعْنًى فِي نَفْسِهَا غَيْرَ مُقْتَرِنٍ بِزَمَانٍ فَهِيَ اسْمٌ).

[2] This third bullet by itself is the definition found in more modern texts like *al-Nahw al-Wadih*. See, for example, 'Ali al-Jaarim & Mustafa Ameen, *al-Nahw al-Wadih li al-Madaris al-Ibtida'iyyah*, (Cairo: Dar al-Ma'arif, n.d.), vol. 1, 16. Their definition of اِسْمٌ is as follows:

(اَلْاِسْمُ: كُلُّ لَفْظٍ يُسَمَّى بِهِ إِنْسَانٌ أَوْ حَيَوَانٌ أَوْ نَبَاتٌ أَوْ جَمَادٌ أَوْ أَيُّ شَيْءٍ آخَرَ).

فِعْلٌ – Verb:

- It is that كَلِمَةٌ whose meaning can be understood without the need to combine it with another word.
- It has one of the three tenses: past, present, or future.[3]
- It denotes an action.[4]

e.g.   ضَرَبَ   He hit.   نَصَرَ   He helped.

Note: A فِعْلٌ can never have a تَنْوِيْنٌ (*tanween*) or an ال.

حَرْفٌ – Particle:

It is that كَلِمَةٌ whose meaning cannot be understood without joining an اِسْمٌ or a فِعْلٌ or both to it.

e.g.   مِنْ   (from)
       عَلَى   (on top)

EXERCISES

1. State with reason whether the following words are اِسْمٌ ، فِعْلٌ or حَرْفٌ.

   i. جَلَسَ (He sat.)   iii. بِنْتٌ (girl)
   ii. وَ   (and)   iv. كَسَرَ (He broke.)

2. Find the meaning and the plural of the following nouns using a dictionary.

   i. قَلَمٌ   iii. كِتَابٌ
   ii. فَصْلٌ   iv. سَبُّوْرَةٌ

---

[3] The first two bullets combine to form the classical definition of فِعْلٌ. See *Sharh ibn 'Aqil*, vol. 1, 15.

[4] The last two bullets combine to form the definition of فِعْلٌ as given in *al-Nahw al-Wadih*. See *al-Nahw al-Wadih, Ibtida'iyyah*, vol. 1, 16.

Section 1.3

أَقْسَامُ الاِسْمِ – Types of Noun

اِسْمٌ is of three types:

1. جَامِدٌ – Primary Noun: It is that اِسْمٌ which is neither derived from another word nor is any word derived from it.

    e.g.   فَرَسٌ   horse   بِنْتٌ   girl

2. مَصْدَرٌ – Root Noun: It is that اِسْمٌ from which many words are derived.

    e.g.   ضَرْبٌ   to hit   نَصْرٌ   to help

3. مُشْتَقٌّ – Derived Noun: It is that اِسْمٌ which is derived from a *masdar*.

    e.g.   ضَارِبٌ   hitter   مَنْصُورٌ   the helped

أَقْسَامُ الْفِعْلِ – Types of Verb

فِعْلٌ is of four types:

1.	اَلْمَاضِيْ	Past tense	e.g.	ضَرَبَ	He hit.
2.	اَلْمُضَارِعُ	Present and Future tense	e.g.	يَضْرِبُ	He is hitting or will hit.
3.	اَلْأَمْرُ	Positive Command/ Imperative	e.g.	اِضْرِبْ	Hit!
4.	اَلنَّهْيُ	Negative Command/ Prohibitive	e.g.	لَا تَضْرِبْ	Don't hit!

أَقْسَامُ الْحَرْفِ – Types of Particle

حَرْفٌ is of two types:

1. عَامِلٌ – Causative Particle: It is that حَرْفٌ, which causes إِعْرَابٌ change in the word after it.

    e.g.   زَيْدٌ فِي الْمَسْجِدِ   Zayd is in the mosque.

2. غَيْرُ الْعَامِلِ – Non-Causative: It is that حَرْفٌ, which does not cause إِعْرَابٌ change in the word after it.

    e.g.   ثُمَّ   then   وَ   and

EXERCISES

1. Correct the following words (stating a reason) and give its meaning.

    i. اَلْبَيْتْ   iii. اَلْوَرَقٌ

    ii. اَلْفَتَحَ   iv. سَمِعٌ

2. Find the meaning and the plural of the following nouns using a dictionary.

    i. بُسْتَانٌ   iii. بَابٌ

    ii. قَمَرٌ   iv. كَلْبٌ

3. Translate the following sentences, and identify the different types of verbs in them.

    i. فَتَحَ خَالِدٌ الشُّبَّاكَ   iii. اُكْتُبْ رِسَالَةً

    ii. يَدْرُسُ أَحْمَدُ فِي الْمَدْرَسَةِ   iv. لَا تَقْرَأْ ذٰلِكَ الْكِتَابَ

Section 1.4
اَلْجُمَلُ وَ الْمُرَكَّبَاتُ – Sentences and Phrases

مُرَكَّبٌ is of two types: مُرَكَّبٌ مُفِيدٌ and مُرَكَّبٌ غَيْرُ مُفِيدٍ.

- مُرَكَّبٌ مُفِيدٌ is also called جُمْلَةٌ مُفِيدَةٌ, مُرَكَّبٌ تَامٌّ and كَلَامٌ تَامٌّ. This is a complete sentence. Often, it is just called كَلَامٌ.
- مُرَكَّبٌ غَيْرُ مُفِيدٍ is also called جُمْلَةٌ غَيْرُ مُفِيدَةٍ, مُرَكَّبٌ نَاقِصٌ and كَلَامٌ نَاقِصٌ. This is a phrase, i.e., an incomplete sentence.

From now onwards, when we use "sentence," we will be referring to complete sentences; and when we use "phrase," we will be referring to incomplete sentences.

Types of Sentences
There are two types of sentences:
A. جُمْلَةٌ خَبَرِيَّةٌ: It is that sentence, which has the possibility of being true or false.
B. جُمْلَةٌ إِنْشَائِيَّةٌ: It is that sentence, which does not have the possibility of being true or false.

Section 1.4.1
أَقْسَامُ الْجُمْلَةِ الْخَبَرِيَّةِ

جُمْلَةٌ خَبَرِيَّةٌ is of two types:

1. جُمْلَةٌ اِسْمِيَّةٌ خَبَرِيَّةٌ – **Nominal Sentence:**

    Definition: It is that sentence, which begins with a noun.
    - The second part of the sentence can be a noun or a verb.
    - The first part of the sentence is called مُبْتَدَأٌ (subject) or مُسْنَدٌ إِلَيْهِ (the word about which information is being given).
    - The second part of the sentence is called خَبَرٌ (predicate) or مُسْنَدٌ (the word giving the information).
    - The مُبْتَدَأٌ is generally مَعْرِفَةٌ and the خَبَرٌ generally نَكِرَةٌ.
    - Both parts (مُبْتَدَأٌ and خَبَرٌ) are مَرْفُوعٌ.

    Sentence Analysis

    اَلْبَيْتُ نَظِيفٌ The house is clean.
    مُبْتَدَأٌ + خَبَرٌ = جُمْلَةٌ اِسْمِيَّةٌ خَبَرِيَّةٌ

Note: A sentence may have more than one خَبَرٌ.

Sentence Analysis

The man is tall and strong. اَلرَّجُلُ طَوِيلٌ قَوِيٌّ

مُبْتَدَأٌ + خَبَرٌ 1 + خَبَرٌ 2 = جُمْلَةٌ اِسْمِيَّةٌ خَبَرِيَّةٌ

2. **جُمْلَةٌ فِعْلِيَّةٌ خَبَرِيَّةٌ – Verbal Sentence:**

   Definition: It is that sentence, which begins with a verb.

   - The first part of the sentence is called فِعْلٌ or مُسْنَدٌ.
   - The second part of the sentence is called فَاعِلٌ or مُسْنَدٌ إِلَيْهِ and is always مَرْفُوعٌ.

Sentence Analysis

Zayd sat. جَلَسَ زَيْدٌ

فِعْلٌ + فَاعِلٌ = جُمْلَةٌ فِعْلِيَّةٌ خَبَرِيَّةٌ

Note: In the above example, the verb is اَلْفِعْلُ اللَّازِمُ i.e. it is a verb whose meaning can be understood without a مَفْعُولٌ.

Note: If the verb is اَلْفِعْلُ الْمُتَعَدِّيُّ i.e. a verb whose meaning cannot be fully understood without a مَفْعُولٌ, then a مَفْعُولٌ will be added and will be مَنْصُوبٌ.

Sentence Analysis

Allah created the sky. خَلَقَ اللهُ السَّمَاءَ

فِعْلٌ + فَاعِلٌ + مَفْعُولٌ = جُمْلَةٌ فِعْلِيَّةٌ خَبَرِيَّةٌ

EXERCISES[5]

1. Translate, fill in the *i'raab*, and analyze the following sentences.

   i. المعلم حاضر   ii. البستان جميل   iii. فتح محمدٍ الباب

   iv. المدرسة كبيرة نظيفة   v. وقف الرجل   vi. الرجل وقف

2. What is the difference between (v) and (vi) above?

---

[5] For more examples and exercise, please refer to *al-Nahw al-Wadih, Ibtida'iyyah*, vol. 1, 11-19 & 36-46.

Section 1.4.2

جُمْلَةٌ إِنْشَائِيَّةٌ is of ten types:

1. اَلْأَمْرُ — Positive Command — e.g. اِضْرِبْ — Hit!
2. اَلنَّهْيُ — Negative Command — e.g. لَا تَضْرِبْ — Don't Hit!
3. اَلْاِسْتِفْهَامُ — Interrogative — e.g. هَلْ ضَرَبَ زَيْدٌ؟ — Did Zayd hit?
4. اَلتَّمَنِّي — Desire — e.g. لَيْتَ الشَّبَابَ عَائِدٌ! — I wish youth would return.

   Note: لَيْتَ is generally used for something unattainable.

5. اَلتَّرَجِّي — Hope — e.g. لَعَلَّ الْاِمْتِحَانَ سَهْلٌ — Hopefully, the examination will be easy.

   Note: لَعَلَّ is generally used for something attainable.

6. اَلنِّدَاءُ — Exclamation — e.g. يَا اَللّٰهُ! — O Allah!
7. اَلْعَرْضُ — Request/Offer — e.g. أَلَا تَأْتِينِي فَأُعْطِيَكَ دِينَارًا؟ — Will you not come to me so that I may give you a *dinar*?

   Note: اَلْعَرْضُ is a mere request; no answer is anticipated.

8. اَلْقَسَمُ — Oath — e.g. وَاللهِ! — By Allah!
9. اَلتَّعَجُّبُ — Amazement — e.g. مَا أَحْسَنَ زَيْدًا! — How good Zayd is!
10. اَلْعُقُودُ — Transaction — e.g. The seller says بِعْتُ هٰذَا الْكِتَابَ – I sold this book. and the buyer says اِشْتَرَيْتُهُ – I bought it.

    Note: The sentences for اَلْعُقُودُ are in reality خَبَرِيَّةٌ. However, Islamic law recognizes them as إِنْشَائِيَّةٌ with respect to all contracts, and requires that they (past tense verbal sentences) be used to convey definiteness.

Sentence Analysis:

هَلْ ضَرَبَ زَيْدٌ؟ — Did Zayd hit?

حَرْفُ الْاِسْتِفْهَامِ + فِعْلٌ + فَاعِلٌ = جُمْلَةٌ إِنْشَائِيَّةٌ

EXERCISE

1. State what type of جُمْلَةٌ إِنْشَائِيَّةٌ are the following sentences.

   i. يَا إِبْرَاهِيْمُ!
   ii. اِسْمَعْ
   iii. كَيْفَ حَالُكَ؟
   iv. لَا تَدْخُلْ

Section 1.4.3
Types of Phrases - أَقْسَامُ الْمُرَكَّبِ النَّاقِصِ

Phrases are of five types:

1. اَلْمُرَكَّبُ التَّوْصِيفِيُّ – **Descriptive Phrase:**[6] It is a phrase in which one word describes the other.
   - The describing word is called صِفَةٌ.
   - The object being described is called مَوْصُوْفٌ.
   - The مَوْصُوْفٌ and صِفَةٌ must correspond in four things:
     1. I'raab.
     2. Gender i.e. being masculine or feminine.
     3. Number i.e. being singular, dual or plural.
     4. Being *ma'rifah* or *nakirah*.

   For example,

صَالِحٌ	رَجُلٌ	a righteous man
صِفَةٌ	مَوْصُوْفٌ	

اَلْعَاقِلَةُ	اَلْبِنْتُ	the intelligent/wise girl
صِفَةٌ	مَوْصُوْفٌ	

2. اَلْمُرَكَّبُ الْإِضَافِيُّ – **Possessive Phrase:** It is a phrase in which the first word (مُضَافٌ) is attributed to the second one (مُضَافٌ إِلَيْهِ). In some cases, this means that the second word owns or possesses the first.
   - The مُضَافٌ never gets an ال or a تَنْوِيْنٌ.
   - The مُضَافٌ إِلَيْهِ is always مَجْرُوْرٌ.

   e.g.

زَيْدٍ	كِتَابُ	Zayd's book
مُضَافٌ إِلَيْهِ	مُضَافٌ	

   - The *i'raab* of the مُضَافٌ will be according to the عَامِلٌ governing it. For example,

   زَيْدٍ   كِتَابَ   وَجَدْتُ   I found Zayd's book.
   مُضَافٌ إِلَيْهِ   مُضَافٌ   فَاعِلٌ مَعَ فَاعِلِهِ
   مَفْعُوْلٌ بِهِ

---

[6] For more examples and exercises, please refer to *al-Nahw al-Wadih, Ibtida'iyyah*, vol. 1, 82-86.

Notes:

1. Sometimes many مُضَاف, مُضَاف إِلَيْهِ are found in one single phrase. For example,

   the door of the man's house   بَابٌ   بَيْتٍ   الرَّجُلِ
   مُضَافٌ   مُضَافٌ إِلَيْهِ وَمُضَافٌ   مُضَافٌ إِلَيْهِ

2. If a صِفَةٌ of the مُضَافٌ is brought, it should come immediately after the مُضَافٌ إِلَيْهِ with an ال and should have the same *i'raab* as that of the مُضَافٌ. For example,

   the new door of the house   بَابُ   الْبَيْتِ   الْجَدِيدُ
   مُضَافٌ   مُضَافٌ إِلَيْهِ   صِفَةُ الْمُضَافِ

3. If a صِفَةٌ of the مُضَافٌ إِلَيْهِ is brought, it should come immediately after it (مُضَافٌ إِلَيْهِ), and it should correspond to it (مُضَافٌ إِلَيْهِ) i.e. in the four aspects mentioned earlier. For example,

   the door of the new house   بَابُ   الْبَيْتِ   الْجَدِيدِ
   مُضَافٌ   مَوْصُوفٌ   صِفَةٌ
   مُضَافٌ إِلَيْهِ

3. اَلْمُرَكَّبُ الْإِشَارِيُّ – **Demonstrative Phrase:** It is a phrase in which one noun (اِسْمُ الْإِشَارَةِ) points towards another noun (مُشَارٌ إِلَيْهِ).

   - The مُشَارٌ إِلَيْهِ must have an ال.

     e.g.   هٰذَا   الرَّجُلُ   This man
            اِسْمُ الْإِشَارَةِ   مُشَارٌ إِلَيْهِ

   Note: If the مُشَارٌ إِلَيْهِ does not have an ال, it would be a complete sentence.

     e.g.   هٰذَا   رَجُلٌ   This is a man.
            مُبْتَدَأٌ + خَبَرٌ = جُمْلَةٌ اِسْمِيَّةٌ

4. اَلْمُرَكَّبُ الْبِنَائِيُّ / اَلْمُرَكَّبُ الْعَدَدِيُّ – **Numerical Phrase:** It is a phrase in which two numerals are joined to form a single word (number).

   - A حَرْفٌ originally linked the two.
     e.g. أَحَدَ عَشَرَ (eleven)   It was originally أَحَدٌ وَعَشْرٌ.
   - This phrase is found only in numbers 11-19.
     e.g. (19) تِسْعَ عَشَرَ, … (13) ثَلَاثَ عَشَرَ, (12) اِثْنَا عَشَرَ, (11) أَحَدَ عَشَرَ.

- Both parts of this phrase will always be مَفْتُوحٌ except the number 12 (اِثْنَا عَشَرَ).

    e.g. (حَالَةُ النَّصْبِ) رَأَيْتُ أَحَدَ عَشَرَ رَجُلًا   (حَالَةُ الرَّفْعِ) جَاءَ أَحَدَ عَشَرَ رَجُلًا
    I saw eleven men.   Eleven men came.
    (حَالَةُ الْجَرِّ) مَرَرْتُ بِأَحَدَ عَشَرَ رَجُلًا
    I passed by eleven men.

- As for number 12, its second part is always مَفْتُوحٌ while the first part changes. Thus, in حَالَةُ الرَّفْعِ, it is written as اِثْنَا عَشَرَ, with an ا at the end of the first part. However, in حَالَةُ النَّصْبِ and حَالَةُ الْجَرِّ, the first part is given a ي in place of the ا (اِثْنَيْ عَشَرَ).

    e.g. (حَالَةُ النَّصْبِ) رَأَيْتُ اِثْنَيْ عَشَرَ رَجُلًا   (حَالَةُ الرَّفْعِ) جَاءَ اِثْنَا عَشَرَ رَجُلًا
    I saw twelve men.   Twelve men came.
    (حَالَةُ الْجَرِّ) مَرَرْتُ بِاثْنَيْ عَشَرَ رَجُلًا
    I passed by twelve men.

5. ٱلْمُرَكَّبُ مَنْعُ الصَّرْفِ – **Indeclinable Phrase**: It is a phrase in which two words are joined to form a single word.
    - The first part of this phrase is always مَفْتُوحٌ.
    - The second part changes according to the عَامِلٌ.

Examples:

1. حَضَرَمَوْتُ is the name of a region in Yemen. It is composed of two words حَضَرَ and مَوْتُ. حَضَرَ is a verb, which means "he/it became present" and مَوْتُ is a noun, which means "death." Thus, literally, حَضَرَمَوْتُ means "[a place where] death became present."

2. بَعْلَبَكُّ is a city in Lebanon. It is composed of two words بَعْلُ and بَكُّ. بَعْلُ was the name of an idol and بَكُّ was the name of a king.

Note: The above mentioned various types of phrases/incomplete sentences form part of a complete sentence.

Example 1   ٱلْأَمِينُ   ٱلتَّاجِرُ   رَبِحَ   The trustworthy/honest trader gained profit.

مَوْصُوفٌ + صِفَةٌ

فِعْلٌ + فَاعِلٌ = جُمْلَةٌ فِعْلِيَّةٌ خَبَرِيَّةٌ

11

Example 2   كُلُّ   فَاعِلٍ   مَرْفُوعٌ   Every *faa'il* is *marfoo'*
و   كُلُّ   مَفْعُولٍ   مَنْصُوبٌ   and every *maf'ool* is *mansoob*.

مُضَافٌ + مُضَافٌ إِلَيْهِ

مُبْتَدَأٌ + خَبَرٌ = جُمْلَةٌ اِسْمِيَّةٌ خَبَرِيَّةٌ

Example 3   اِشْتَرَيْتُ   هَذَا   الْكِتَابَ   I bought this book.

اِسْمُ الْإِشَارَةِ + مُشَارٌ إِلَيْهِ

فِعْلٌ مَعَ فَاعِلِهِ + مَفْعُولٌ = جُمْلَةٌ فِعْلِيَّةٌ خَبَرِيَّةٌ

Example 4   جَاءَ   أَرْبَعَةَ عَشَرَ رَجُلًا   Fourteen men came.

فِعْلٌ + فَاعِلٌ = جُمْلَةٌ فِعْلِيَّةٌ خَبَرِيَّةٌ

Example 5   هَذِهِ   بَعْلَبَكُّ   This is Ba'labakk.

مُبْتَدَأٌ + خَبَرٌ = جُمْلَةٌ اِسْمِيَّةٌ خَبَرِيَّةٌ

EXERCISES

1. Translate, fill in the *i'raab* and analyze the following phrases.

   i. سيارة الرجل   v. الوردة الجميلة
   ii. أربع عشر   vi. قلم رخيص
   iii. باب فصل المدرسة   vii. معديكرب
   iv. قلم الرجل الطويل   viii. ذلك الكتاب

2. What is the difference between the following sentences?

   i. غُلَامٌ عَاقِلٌ   and   غُلَامٌ عَاقِلٌ
   ii. هذه تفاحة   and   هذه التفاحة
   iii. نافذة السيارة الكبيرةُ and   نافذة السيارة الكبيرةُ
   iv. الثوب نظيف   and   الثوب النظيف

3. Correct the following and state the reason(s).

   i. وَلَدٌ القبيحٌ   iii. المعلمُ المدرسةِ

   ii. الرجلان الطويل   iv. ثمانيةُ عَشَرٍ

4. Translate, fill in the *i'raab* and analyze the following.

   i. باب فضل قيام ليلة القدر

Section 1.4.4
Additional Notes About جُمْلَةٌ اِسْمِيَّةٌ

1. Sometimes, the خَبَرٌ is not mentioned, in which case it will be regarded as hidden (مُقَدَّرٌ).[7]

   e.g. اَلْإِمَامُ فِي الْمَسْجِدِ   The Imam is in the mosque.

2. The خَبَرٌ can be a complete sentence.

   Example 1:   زَيْدٌ أَبُوهُ عَالِمٌ   Zayd's father is knowledgeable.

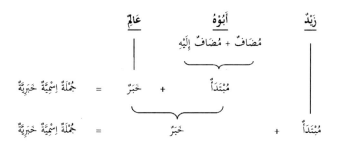

   Example 2:   زَيْدٌ أَكَلَ الطَّعَامَ   Zayd ate the food.

EXERCISE

1. Translate, fill in the *i'raab*, and analyze the following sentences.

   i. القلم في الفصل   ii. الثور يحرث الأرض

---

[7] However, generally, to simplify matters, the مُتَعَلِّقٌ is taken to be خَبَرٌ. See Mawlana Hasan Dockrat, *A Simplified Arabic Grammar*, (Azaadvillle: Madrasa Arabia Islamia, 2003), 37.

Summary

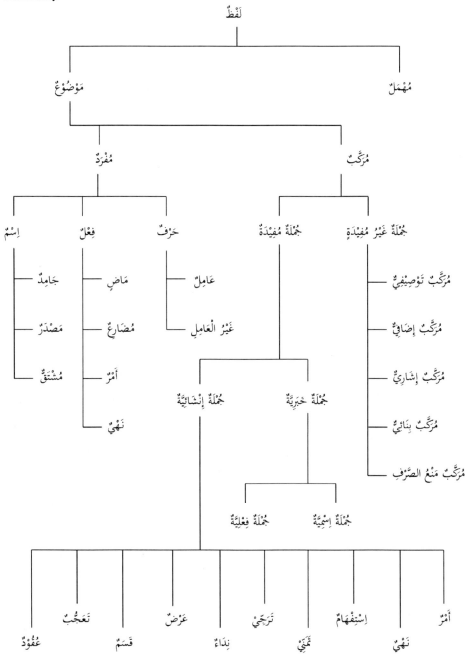

Section 1.5

عَلَامَاتُ الْاِسْمِ – Signs of a Noun:

1.	It is preceded by an ال.	e.g.	اَلرَّجُلُ	the man
2.	It accepts جَرٌّ.	e.g.	فِيْ بَيْتِ زَيْدٍ الْجَدِيْدِ	in Zayd's new house
3.	There is *tanween* on the last letter.	e.g.	رَجُلٌ	a man
4.	It ends with a round ة.	e.g.	كَلِمَةٌ	a word
5.	It is a dual (تَثْنِيَةٌ).[8]	e.g.	رَجُلَانِ	two men
6.	It is a plural (جَمْعٌ).	e.g.	رِجَالٌ	men
7.	It is a (فَاعِلٌ or مُبْتَدَأٌ مُسْنَدٌ إِلَيْهِ).	e.g.	اَلرَّجُلُ قَوِيٌّ	The man is strong.
		e.g.	جَلَسَ زَيْدٌ	Zayd sat.
8.	It is مُضَافٌ.	e.g.	كِتَابُ زَيْدٍ	book of Zayd
9.	It is مَوْصُوْفٌ.	e.g.	رَجُلٌ طَوِيْلٌ	tall man
10.	It is مُنَادَى.	e.g.	يَا رَجُلُ	O man!
11.	It is مُصَغَّرٌ.	e.g.	رُجَيْلٌ	a little man
12.	It is مَنْسُوْبٌ.	e.g.	مَكِّيٌّ	a Makkan

عَلَامَاتُ الْفِعْلِ – Signs of a Verb:

1.	It is preceded by قَدْ.	e.g.	قَدْ خَرَجَ	He has gone out.
2.	It is preceded by سَ.	e.g.	سَيَخْرُجُ	He will soon go out.
3.	It is preceded by سَوْفَ.	e.g.	سَوْفَ يَخْرُجُ	He will go out after a while.
4.	It is preceded by حَرْفُ جَزْمٍ.	e.g.	لَمْ يَخْرُجْ	He did not go out.
5.	It is preceded by حَرْفُ نَصْبٍ.	e.g.	لَنْ يَخْرُجَ	He will never go out.
6.	It has a hidden ضَمِيْرٌ.	e.g.	خَرَجَ	He went out.
7.	It is an imperative (أَمْرٌ).	e.g.	أُخْرُجْ	Go out.
8.	It is a prohibitive (نَهْيٌ).	e.g.	لَا تَخْرُجْ	Do not go out.
9.	It has *taa saakin* (تْ) at the end.	e.g.	أَكَلَتْ	She ate.

عَلَامَةُ الْحَرْفِ – Sign of a Particle:

That word which has no sign of a noun or verb is a particle (a particle has no sign of its own).

---

[8] Verbs are said to be dual and plural with respect to their doers (فَاعِلٌ). The action is one. Thus, duality and plurality are signs of a noun and not a verb.

Section 1.5.1
General Notes

1. The indefiniteness of a noun (اِسْمٌ) is indicated by a *tanween*. Such a noun is called نَكِرَةٌ.

    e.g. بَيْتٌ   a house (any house)

2. The definiteness of a noun is indicated by an ال. Such a noun is called مَعْرِفَةٌ.

    e.g. اَلْبَيْتُ   the house (a specific house)

3. A noun can never have a *tanween* and an ال at the same time.

    e.g. اَلْبَيْتٌ   is incorrect.

4. When the last letter of a word and the first letter of the following word have *sukoon* (ْ), it is called اِجْتِمَاعُ السَّاكِنَيْنِ (the meeting of two *sukoons*). In this case, the first *sukoon* is generally changed to a *kasrah*.

    e.g. ضَرَبَتْ الْبِنْتُ will become ضَرَبَتِ الْبِنْتُ. The هَمْزَةُ الْوَصْلِ before the ل will not be pronounced.

    In some case, the first *sukoon* is changed to a *fathah*.

    e.g. مِنْ الْيَابَانِ (from Japan) will become مِنَ الْيَابَانِ.

    In some cases, the first *sukoon* is changed to *dammah*.

    e.g. فَهِمْتُمْ الدَّرْسَ (you understood the lesson) will become فَهِمْتُمُ الدَّرْسَ.

5. When an ال appears before a noun, which begins with a letter from اَلْحُرُوفُ الشَّمْسِيَّةُ (sun letters) then the ل of ال must not be pronounced. The ل of ال will not get a *sukoon*. Instead the حَرْفٌ شَمْسِيٌّ will get a *tashdeed*.

    e.g. اَلشَّجَرَةُ the tree   اَلشَّمْسُ the sun

    اَلْحُرُوفُ الشَّمْسِيَّةُ - ن ل ظ ط ض ص ش س ز ر ذ د ث ت

6. The remaining letters are known as اَلْحُرُوفُ الْقَمَرِيَّةُ (moon letters). In these, the ل of ال will get a *sukoon* and will be pronounced. The حَرْفٌ قَمَرِيٌّ will not get a *tashdeed*.

    e.g. اَلْقَلَمُ the pen   اَلْقَمَرُ the moon

7. Generally, a noun ending with a round ة (اَلتَّاءُ الْمَرْبُوطَةُ) is a feminine (مُؤَنَّثٌ) noun.

    e.g. سَبُّورَةٌ   blackboard

8. The صِفَةٌ – اِسْمُ الْإِشَارَةِ – اَلْاِسْمُ الْمَوْصُولُ – فِعْلٌ – خَبَرٌ etc. of a غَيْرُ الْعَاقِلِ (non-human) plural will generally be وَاحِدٌ مُؤَنَّثٌ.

e.g.	أَصْنَامٌ كَثِيرَةٌ	many idols	أَلْأَصْنَامُ لَا تَنْفَعُ The idols do not benefit.
	هٰذِهِ الْأَصْنَامُ	these idols	أَلْكِلَابُ الْحَارِسَةُ جَالِسَةٌ The guard dogs are sitting.
	كَانَتِ الْبُيُوتُ كَثِيرَةً		The houses were many.

9. When writing a noun ending with two *fathahs* (◌َ), an *alif* (ا) must be added at the end.

    e.g.   زَيْدًا

However, If there is a round ة (اَلتَّاءُ الْمَرْبُوطَةُ) at the end of such a word, *alif* should not be added.

    e.g.   رِسَالَةً

Section 1.6
اَلضَّمَائِرُ – Personal Pronouns

Definition: ضَمَائِرُ (singular: ضَمِيرٌ) are those words, which are used in place of names and refer to the speaker (مُتَكَلِّمٌ) or the second person (حَاضِرٌ) or the third person (غَائِبٌ).

Table 1.1
اَلضَّمَائِرُ – Personal Pronouns

Unattached Form (مُنْفَصِلٌ)		Attached Form (مُتَّصِلٌ)		
هُوَ	He (one male), it	ہُ	his, its, him	وَاحِدٌ مُذَكَّرٌ غَائِبٌ
هُمَا	They (two males)	هُمَا	their, them	تَثْنِيَةٌ مُذَكَّرٌ غَائِبٌ
هُمْ	They (many males)	هُمْ	their, them	جَمْعٌ مُذَكَّرٌ غَائِبٌ
هِيَ	She (one female), it	هَا	her, its	وَاحِدٌ مُؤَنَّثٌ غَائِبٌ
هُمَا	They (two females)	هُمَا	their, them	تَثْنِيَةٌ مُؤَنَّثٌ غَائِبٌ
هُنَّ	They (many females)	هُنَّ	their, them	جَمْعٌ مُؤَنَّثٌ غَائِبٌ
أَنْتَ	You (one male)	كَ	your	وَاحِدٌ مُذَكَّرٌ حَاضِرٌ
أَنْتُمَا	You (two males)	كُمَا	your	تَثْنِيَةٌ مُذَكَّرٌ حَاضِرٌ
أَنْتُمْ	You (many males)	كُمْ	your	جَمْعٌ مُذَكَّرٌ حَاضِرٌ
أَنْتِ	You (one female)	كِ	your	وَاحِدٌ مُؤَنَّثٌ حَاضِرٌ
أَنْتُمَا	You (two females)	كُمَا	your	تَثْنِيَةٌ مُؤَنَّثٌ حَاضِرٌ
أَنْتُنَّ	You (many females)	كُنَّ	your	جَمْعٌ مُؤَنَّثٌ حَاضِرٌ
أَنَا	I (one male or female)	ـِي، نِي	my, mine, me	وَاحِدٌ مُتَكَلِّمٌ (مُذَكَّرٌ وَمُؤَنَّثٌ)
نَحْنُ	We (many males or females)	نَا	our	تَثْنِيَةٌ وَجَمْعٌ مُتَكَلِّمٌ (مُذَكَّرٌ وَمُؤَنَّثٌ)

In the unattached form, these *dameers* can appear as *mubtada*, *faa'il*, etc. In the attached form, they can appear as *maf'ool* or *mudaaf ilayhi*. For more details, see section 2.4.1.

| e.g. | هُوَ زَيْدٌ | He is Zayd. | قَلَمُكَ | your pen |
| | أَنَا طَالِبٌ | I am a student. | نَصَرْتُهَا | I helped her. |

---

[9] Sometimes, a ن (نُونُ الْوِقَايَةِ) is added before the ضَمِيرٌ يَاء to protect an *i'raab* as in ضَرَبَنِي, which would otherwise be incorrectly read as ضَرَبِي (the لَامُ الْكَلِمَةِ of الْفِعْلُ الْمَاضِي is مَبْنِيٌّ عَلَى الْفَتْحِ).

Section 1.7[10]

اَلْحُرُوفُ الْجَارَّةُ – Prepositions

Effect: A حَرْفُ جَرٍّ gives a جَرٌّ to the noun it enters upon, which is then known as مَجْرُورٌ.

Table 1.2
اَلْحُرُوفُ الْجَارَّةُ – Prepositions

حَرْفُ جَرٍّ		Meaning	Example	
1.	بِ	with	كَتَبْتُ بِالْقَلَمِ	I wrote with the pen.
2.	تَ	by (for oath)	تَاللهِ	By Allah!
3.	كَ	like	زَيْدٌ كَالْأَسَدِ	Zayd is like a lion.
4.	لِ	for	اَلْحَمْدُ لِلهِ	All praise is for Allah.
5.	وَ	by (oath)	وَاللهِ	By Allah!
6.	مُنْذُ	since	مَا رَأَيْتُهُ مُنْذُ أُسْبُوعٍ	I have not seen him since a week.
7.	مُذْ	since/for	مَا رَأَيْتُهُ مُذْ أَرْبَعَةِ أَيَّامٍ	I have not see him for four days.
8.	خَلَا	besides, except	جَاءَ النَّاسُ خَلَا زَيْدٍ	The people came except Zayd.
9.	رُبَّ	many a...	رُبَّ عَالِمٍ يَعْمَلُ بِعِلْمِهِ	Many a learned person acts on his knowledge.
10.	حَاشَا	besides, except	جَاءَ النَّاسُ حَاشَا زَيْدٍ	The people came except Zayd.
11.	مِنْ	from	رَجَعْتُ مِنَ السَّفَرِ	I returned from the journey.
12.	عَدَا	besides, except	جَاءَ النَّاسُ عَدَا زَيْدٍ	The people came except Zayd.
13.	فِي	in, regarding	زَيْدٌ فِي الْبَيْتِ	Zayd is in the house.
14.	عَنْ	from, regarding	سَأَلَ الطَّبِيبُ عَنِ الْمَرِيضِ	The doctor asked about the patient.
15.	عَلَى	on	اَلثَّوْبُ عَلَى الْكُرْسِيِّ	The cloth/clothes is/are on the chair.
16.	حَتَّى	up to, until	نِمْتُ حَتَّى الصُّبْحِ	I slept till dawn.
17.	إِلَى	up to, towards	سَافَرْتُ إِلَى الْمَدِينَةِ	I travelled to Madinah.

Example 1: اَلنَّحْوُ فِي الْكَلَامِ كَالْمِلْحِ فِي الطَّعَامِ   Grammar in speech is like salt in food.

---

[10] For more examples and exercises, please refer to *al-Nahw al-Wadih, Ibtida'iyyah*, vol. 1, 76-81.

Example 2 with Sentence Analysis:

I wrote with the pen.

Note: Together, the حَرْفُ جَرٍّ and مَجْرُورٌ are known as مُتَعَلَّقٌ (connected) of the خَبَرٌ in جُمْلَةٌ اِسْمِيَّةٌ (there is more detail to this, and will follow later), and of the فِعْلٌ in جُمْلَةٌ فِعْلِيَّةٌ.

EXERCISE

1. Translate, fill in the *i'raab* and analyze the following sentences.

   i. المسجد قريب من بيت زيد

   ii. نزل المطر من السماء

   iii. الكتب على المنضدة

   iv. زينب جالسة على الكرسي في الحجرة

Section 1.8[11]
اَلْحُرُوفُ الْمُشَبَّهَةُ بِالْفِعْلِ (also called (إِنَّ وَأَخَوَاتُهَا)) – Those Particles That Resemble the Verb

- These are called اَلْحُرُوفُ الْمُشَبَّهَةُ بِالْفِعْلِ because like اَلْفِعْلُ الْمُتَعَدِّيْ, they also govern two words.
- These حُرُوفٌ appear before a مُبْتَدَأ and خَبَر (جُمْلَةٌ اِسْمِيَّةٌ).

Effect: Such a particle gives a نَصْبٌ to the مُبْتَدَأ which is then known as اِسْمُ إِنَّ (or اِسْمُ أَنَّ and so on) and a رَفْعٌ to the خَبَر which is then known as خَبَرُ إِنَّ (or خَبَرُ أَنَّ and so on).

Table 1.3
اَلْحُرُوفُ الْمُشَبَّهَةُ بِالْفِعْلِ – Those Particles That Resemble the Verb

		Meaning		Example
1.	إِنَّ	certainly, verily, indeed	إِنَّ اللهَ عَلِيْمٌ	Verily Allah is All-Knowing.
2.	أَنَّ	that	أَعْرِفُ أَنَّ الْاِمْتِحَانَ قَرِيْبٌ	I know that the examination is near.
3.	كَأَنَّ	as if	كَأَنَّ الْبَيْتَ جَدِيْدٌ	It is as if the house is new.
4.	لٰكِنَّ	but, however	اَلْبَيْتُ جَدِيْدٌ لٰكِنَّ الْأَثَاثَ قَدِيْمٌ	The house is new but the furniture is old.
5.	لَيْتَ	if only, I wish	لَيْتَ الشَّبَابَ عَائِدٌ	I wish youth would return.
6.	لَعَلَّ	maybe, hopefully, perhaps	لَعَلَّ الْاِمْتِحَانَ سَهْلٌ	Hopefully, the examination will be easy.

Sentence Analysis:

عَلِيْمٌ   اللهَ   إِنَّ   Indeed, Allah is All-Knowing.
خَبَرُ إِنَّ   اِسْمُ إِنَّ   اَلْحَرْفُ الْمُشَبَّهَةُ بِالْفِعْلِ

Notes:
1. Difference between إِنَّ and أَنَّ:
   a. إِنَّ is generally used at the beginning of a sentence.
   أَنَّ is generally used in the middle of a sentence.

---
[11] For more examples and exercises, please refer to *al-Nahw al-Wadih, Ibtida'iyyah*, vol. 1, 69-75.

b. Sometimes, إِنَّ appears in the middle of a sentence. This happens in the following two cases:

   i. When it is used after a word with root letters ق - و - ل.

      e.g. يَقُوْلُ إِنَّهَا بَقَرَةٌ صَفْرَاءُ   He says, indeed, it is a yellow cow.

   ii. When it is at the beginning of a صِلَةٌ.[12]

      e.g. زُرْتُ الَّذِيْ إِنِّيْ أَحْتَرِمُهُ   I visited the one whom I respect.

2. The خَبَر can be a complete sentence.

   Example 1: إِنَّ زَيْدًا أُمُّهُ صَالِحَةٌ   Indeed, Zayd's mother is pious.

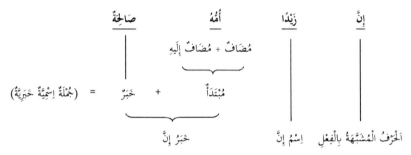

   Example 2: إِنَّ زَيْدًا أَكَلَ الطَّعَامَ   Indeed, Zayd ate the food.

3. If the خَبَر is (جَارٌ وَمَجْرُوْرٌ), then the خَبَر will appear first and the اِسْم second.

   e.g. إِنَّ إِلَيْنَا إِيَابَهُمْ   Indeed, to us is their return.

---

[12] صِلَةٌ will be discussed in Section 2.4.2.

4. When مَا الْكَافَّةُ is joined to any of these حُرُوفٌ, their effect is cancelled.

   e.g. إِنَّمَا إِلٰهُكُمْ إِلٰهٌ وَاحِدٌ   Your god is only one god.

   Note: In this example, the meaning has also changed to "only."

5. إِنَّ by itself conveys emphasis. Sometimes, لَامُ التَّأْكِيدِ can be added before the خَبَر to convey even more emphasis.

   e.g. إِنَّكَ لَرَسُوْلُ اللهِ   Indeed, you are the messenger of Allah.

   إِنِّيْ لَأَعْرِفُ أَخَاكَ   Indeed, I know your brother.

EXCERISE

1. Translate, fill in the *i'raab*, and analyze the following sentences.

   i. لعل المريض نائم   iv. كأن القمر مصباح
   ii. اعلم أن زيدا عاقل   v. ليت القمر طالع
   iii. إن رجلا دخل البيت   vi. إن علينا بيانه

Section 1.9[13]
اَلْأَفْعَالُ النَّاقِصَةُ (also called كَانَ وَأَخَوَاتُهَا) – Auxiliary (Defective) Verbs

- فِعْلٌ نَاقِصٌ is called نَاقِصٌ (incomplete/defective) because even though it is a فِعْلٌ لَازِمٌ, it needs two *ma'mools* (مَعْمُولَيْنِ). The sentence remains incomplete with one مَعْمُولٌ.

  e.g. كَانَ زَيْدٌ   Zayd was (the sentence remains incomplete).

- These verbs enter on a مُبْتَدَأٌ and a خَبَرٌ.

Effect: They give رَفْعٌ to the مُبْتَدَأ, which becomes known as اِسْمُ كَانَ (or اِسْمُ صَارَ and so on) and نَصْبٌ to the خَبَر, which becomes known as خَبَرُ كَانَ (or خَبَرُ صَارَ and so on).

Table 1.4

فِعْلٌ نَاقِصٌ	Meaning	Example	
1. كَانَ	was	كَانَ الْبَيْتُ نَظِيفًا	The house was clean.
2. صَارَ	became	صَارَ الرَّجُلُ غَنِيًّا	The man became wealthy.
3. أَصْبَحَ	happen in the morning OR became	أَصْبَحَ زَيْدٌ مَرِيضًا أَصْبَحَ زَيْدٌ غَنِيًّا	Zayd became ill in the morning. Zayd became rich.
4. أَمْسَى	happen in the evening, became	أَمْسَى الْعَامِلُ مُتْعَبًا	The worker became tired in the evening.
5. أَضْحَى	happen at midmorning, became	أَضْحَى الْغَمَامُ كَثِيفًا	The clouds became dense at mid morning.
6. ظَلَّ	happen during the day, became	ظَلَّ الْمَطَرُ نَازِلًا	It rained the whole day.
7. بَاتَ	happen during the night, became	بَاتَ زَيْدٌ نَائِمًا	Zayd passed the night sleeping.
8. مَا دَامَ	as long as	اِجْلِسْ مَا دَامَ زَيْدٌ جَالِسًا	Sit as long as Zayd is sitting.
9. مَا زَالَ	always, continuously	مَا زَالَ زَيْدٌ مَرِيضًا	Zayd was continuously sick.
10. مَا بَرِحَ	always, continuously	مَا بَرِحَ زَيْدٌ صَائِمًا	Zayd was always fasting.
11. مَا فَتِئَ	always, continuously	مَا فَتِئَ زَيْدٌ نَشِيطًا	Zayd was always active.
12. مَا انْفَكَّ	always, continuously	مَا انْفَكَّ التَّاجِرُ صَادِقًا	The trader was always truthful.
13. لَيْسَ	no, not	لَيْسَ الْخَادِمُ قَوِيًّا	The servant is not strong.

---

[13] For more examples and exercises, please refer to *al-Nahw al-Wadih, Ibtida'iyyah*, vol. 1, 62-68 & vol. 2, 151-155.

Sentence Analysis:

نَظِيفًا	الْبَيْتُ	كَانَ	The house was clean.
خَبَرُ كَانَ	اسْمُ كَانَ	فِعْلٌ نَاقِصٌ	

Notes:

1. When كَانَ is used with مُضَارِعٌ, it gives the meaning of past continuous or past habitual.

   e.g.   كَانَ زَيْدٌ يَكْتُبُ   Zayd was writing/Zayd used to write.

   Note: Here, the خَبَر of كَانَ is a جُمْلَةٌ فِعْلِيَّةٌ. Also, note the two ways it is translated above.

2. كَانَ – صَارَ – أَصْبَحَ – أَمْسَى – أَضْحَى – ظَلَّ – بَاتَ can be used in مُضَارِعٌ and أَمْرٌ as well.

3. مَا زَالَ – مَا بَرِحَ – مَا فَتِئَ – مَا انْفَكَّ can be used in مُضَارِعٌ but not in أَمْرٌ.

4. مَا دَامَ and لَيْسَ have a past tense only (no مُضَارِعٌ or أَمْرٌ).

5. مَا دَامَ must be preceded by another sentence.

6. The خَبَر of لَيْسَ is sometimes prefixed with a بـ.

   e.g.   أَلَيْسَ اللهُ بِأَحْكَمِ الْحَاكِمِينَ   Is Allah not the greatest of rulers/best of judges?

7. If the خَبَر is (جَارٌ وَمَجْرُورٌ), then the خَبَر will appear first and the مُبْتَدَأ second.

   e.g.

سَحَابٌ	فِي السَّمَاءِ	كَانَ	There were clouds in the sky.
اسْمُ كَانَ (مُؤَخَّر)	خَبَرُ كَانَ (مُقَدَّم)	فِعْلٌ نَاقِصٌ	

EXERCISE

1. Translate, fill in the *i'raab*, and analyze the following sentences.

   i. ليس العامل نشيطا

   ii. كان منامه مناما صادقا

   iii. أمسى الغني فقيرا

   iv. نويت الاعتكاف ما دمت في المسجد

   v. صار الكبش سمينا

   vi. لا يزال لسانك رطبا من ذكر الله

   vii. يصبح المداد جافا

CHAPTER 2

اَلْمُعْرَبُ وَ الْمَبْنِيُّ – Declinable and Indeclinable Words

Words are of two types with respect to changes, which may or may not take place at their ends. If the end of a word remains the same in all conditions, it is called مَبْنِيٌّ; and that word whose end changes is called مُعْرَبٌ.

Section 2.1[14]

أَنْوَاعُ الْبِنَاءِ: Those conditions or states (أَحْوَالٌ), which remain unchanged at the end of مَبْنِيٌّ words are four: ضَمٌّ, فَتْحٌ, كَسْرٌ and سُكُونٌ. These are called أَنْوَاعُ الْبِنَاءِ.

أَنْوَاعُ الْإِعْرَابِ: Those conditions or states (أَحْوَالٌ), which occur at the end of مُعْرَبٌ words are four: رَفْعٌ, نَصْبٌ, جَرٌّ, and جَزْمٌ. These are called أَنْوَاعُ الْإِعْرَابِ (اَلْإِعْرَابُ for short). These changes are brought about at the end of a مُعْرَبٌ word in accordance with the requirement of the عَامِلٌ (governing word).

عَلَامَاتُ الْإِعْرَابِ – Signs of *I'raab*

I'raab can be expressed in different ways. These are called عَلَامَاتُ الْإِعْرَابِ (signs of *i'raab*). The two common ones are as follows:

1. اَلْإِعْرَابُ بِالْحَرَكَةِ: These are the basic signs and are the most common. *I'raab* is shown by means of a حَرَكَةٌ i.e. ضَمَّةٌ or فَتْحَةٌ or كَسْرَةٌ or سُكُونٌ (which is the absence of a حَرَكَةٌ).

   e.g.   لَمْ يَضْرِبْ   رَجُلٍ   رَجُلًا   رَجُلٌ

2. اَلْإِعْرَابُ بِالْحُرُوفِ: Sometimes, the *i'raab* is shown by means of any of the حُرُوفُ عِلَّةٍ i.e. و or ا or ي.

   e.g.   أَبِيْكَ   أَبَاكَ   أَبُوْكَ

حَالَاتُ الْمُعْرَبِ – States of *Mu'rab*

As mentioned above, the conditions or states that occur at the end of مُعْرَبٌ words are four. Below, we look at them in more detail.

---

[14] This section is based upon the discussion in *al-Nahw al-Wadih*. See *al-Nahw al-Wadih, Ibdtida'iyyah*, vol. 2, 7-18.

1. حَالَةُ الرَّفْعِ is the condition in which a ضَمَّةٌ or its substitute such as حَرْفُ عِلَّةٍ (و) appears at the end of a word. Such a word is said to be مَرْفُوعٌ.
   e.g. أَخٌ   أَخُوكَ   أَبُو خَالِدٍ

2. حَالَةُ النَّصْبِ is the condition in which a فَتْحَةٌ or its substitute such as حَرْفُ عِلَّةٍ (ا) appears at the end of a word. Such a word is said to be مَنْصُوبٌ.
   e.g. أَخًا   أَخَاكَ   أَبَا خَالِدٍ

3. حَالَةُ الْجَرِّ is the condition in which a كَسْرَةٌ or its substitute such as حَرْفُ عِلَّةٍ (ي) appears at the end of a word. Such a word is said to be مَجْرُورٌ.
   e.g. أَخٍ   أَخِيكَ   أَبِي خَالِدٍ

4. حَالَةُ الْجَزْمِ is the condition in which a سُكُونٌ appears at the end of a word or its substitute (ن in the case of فِعْلٌ مُضَارِعٌ) is dropped from the end. Such a word is said to be مَجْزُومٌ.
   e.g. لَمْ يَضْرِبُوا   لَمْ يَضْرِبْ

Note: It should be remembered that verbs can only be in the state of رَفْعٌ, نَصْبٌ or جَزْمٌ, while nouns can only be in a state of رَفْعٌ, نَصْبٌ, or جَرٌّ.

Difference Between كَسْرٌ – فَتْحٌ – ضَمٌّ and كَسْرَةٌ – فَتْحَةٌ – ضَمَّةٌ

- The words كَسْرٌ – فَتْحٌ – ضَمٌّ are used to describe the states at the end of a مَبْنِيٌّ, e.g. ضَرَبَ has a فَتْحٌ at the end. It is مَبْنِيٌّ عَلَى الْفَتْحِ.
- The words كَسْرَةٌ – فَتْحَةٌ – ضَمَّةٌ are used for all other places where (ُ), (َ) and (ِ) appear.

In other words, (ُ), (َ) and (ِ) are normally called ضَمَّةٌ – فَتْحَةٌ – كَسْرَةٌ, respectively, wherever they occur except when one needs to precisely point out the end of a مَبْنِيٌّ word. Thus, one could say ضَرَبَ has a فَتْحَةٌ on (ض), a فَتْحَةٌ on (ر), and a فَتْحَةٌ on (ب), but one must say (ضَرَبَ) is مَبْنِيٌّ عَلَى الْفَتْحِ.

Section 2.2
اَلْمَبْنِيُّ – Indeclinable Word

As mentioned earlier, a مَبْنِيٌّ is that word whose end remains unchanged in all conditions i.e. irrespective of the requirement of the عَامِلٌ governing it.

e.g.	جَاءَ هٰذَا	رَأَيْتُ هٰذَا	مَرَرْتُ بِهٰذَا
	This came.	I saw this.	I passed by this.

<u>Note</u>: The حَرَكَةٌ at the end of هٰذَا remained constant and did not change according to the عَامِلٌ requirement.

<u>Types of</u> مَبْنِيٌّ:

1. All Particles (حُرُوفٌ) *
2. اَلْفِعْلُ الْمَاضِيْ *
3. اَلْأَمْرُ الْحَاضِرُ الْمَعْرُوْفُ *
4. Those *seeghahs* of فِعْلٌ مُضَارِعٌ that are جَمْعُ مُؤَنَّثٍ (حَاضِرٌ and غَائِبٌ) or have نُوْنُ التَّأْكِيْدِ (ثَقِيْلَةٌ and خَفِيْفَةٌ).
5. Amongst nouns (اَلْأَسْمَاءُ), those whose ends remain constant are called غَيْرُ الْمُتَمَكِّنِ i.e. nouns, which do not give place to changes. These nouns are مَبْنِيٌّ and are recognized by their resemblance with any one of the three types of اَلْمَبْنِيُّ الْأَصْلُ words (حُرُوفٌ or اَلْفِعْلُ الْمَاضِي or اَلْأَمْرُ الْحَاضِرُ الْمَعْرُوْفُ). This resemblance can be in any one of the following ways:

    a. Resemblance in meaning. For example, the noun رُوَيْدَ (give grace/respite) resembles the word أَمْهِلْ, which is اَلْأَمْرُ الْحَاضِرُ الْمَعْرُوْفُ (one of the اَلْمَبْنِيُّ الْأَصْلُ) and has the same meaning.

    b. Resemblance in dependency. For example, the noun هٰذَا (اِسْمُ الْإِشَارَةِ), which is dependent on a مُشَارٌ إِلَيْهِ to give meaning, resembles a حَرْفٌ (one of the اَلْمَبْنِيُّ الْأَصْلُ), which is also dependent on another word to give meaning.

    c. Resemblance in having less than three letters. For example, the noun مَنْ, which is less than three letters, resembles حَرْفٌ (e.g. وَ), which is also generally less than three letters.

    d. Resemblance in having had a حَرْفٌ originally. For example, the noun أَحَدَ عَشَرَ resembles a حَرْفٌ in the sense that originally it contained a حَرْفٌ (أَحَدٌ وَعَشْرٌ).

*These three are known as اَلْمَبْنِيُّ الْأَصْلُ.

[15] اَلْإِعْرَابُ الْمَحَلِّيْ

When a مَبْنِيٌّ word appears in a sentence in a place where it is supposed to be in the state of رَفْعٌ, نَصْبٌ, جَرٌّ, or جَزْمٌ, its end does not change because it is مَبْنِيٌّ. However, it is said that it is in the place of رَفْعٌ, نَصْبٌ, جَرٌّ, or جَزْمٌ (فِيْ مَحَلِّ رَفْعٍ أَوْ نَصْبٍ أَوْ جَرٍّ أَوْ جَزْمٍ), in accordance with its place in the sentence.

For example,

    نَصَرْنَاهُ   We helped him.

Keeping in mind that all pronouns are مَبْنِيٌّ, this sentence will be analyzed as follows:

نَصَرَ is فِعْلٌ مَاضٍ and is مَبْنِيٌّ عَلَى السُّكُوْنِ.

نَا is فَاعِلٌ, and is مَبْنِيٌّ عَلَى السُّكُوْنِ and فِيْ مَحَلِّ رَفْعٍ.

هُ is مَفْعُوْلٌ بِهِ, and is مَبْنِيٌّ عَلَى الضَّمِّ and فِيْ مَحَلِّ نَصْبٍ.

EXERCISE

1. Analyze the following sentences like in the example given above.

   i. قرأتُ هذا الكتاب

  ii. ذهبتَ إلى عمه

 iii. كتابه في بيته

---

[15] For more examples and exercises, please refer to *al-Nahw al-Wadih*, *Ibtida'iyyah*, vol. 2, 35-38.

Section 2.3
اَلْمُعْرَبُ – Declinable Word

As mentioned above, a مُعْرَبٌ is that word whose end accepts any of the *i'raab* according to the requirement of the عَامِلٌ governing it.

e.g.   مَرَرْتُ بِرَجُلٍ   رَأَيْتُ رَجُلًا   جَاءَ رَجُلٌ
        I passed by a man.   I saw a man.   A man came.

Note: The *i'raab* of رجل keep on changing according to the requirement of the عَامِلٌ.

Types of مُعْرَبٌ:

1. Amongst verbs (اَلْأَفْعَالُ), all of the *seeghahs* of فِعْلٌ مُضَارِعٌ besides those of جَمْعُ مُؤَنَّثٍ غَائِبٌ and (حَاضِرٌ) and those with نُونُ التَّأْكِيدِ ثَقِيلَةٌ and خَفِيفَةٌ are مُعْرَبٌ.

2. Amongst nouns (اَلْأَسْمَاءُ), those nouns, which accept *i'raab* changes are مُعْرَبٌ. They are known as مُتَمَكِّنٌ i.e. nouns which give place to *i'raab* changes.

   Note: These nouns will be مُعْرَبٌ only when they are used in a sentence. If not used in a sentence, such a word will be مَبْنِيٌّ. For example, بَيْتٌ on its own, when not part of a sentence, will be مَبْنِيٌّ عَلَى الضَّمِّ.

EXERCISES

1. State with reason whether the following words are مَبْنِيٌّ or مُعْرَبٌ.

   i.   سَمِعَ   v.   يَكْسِرْنَ
   ii.   مُنْذُ   vi.   لٰكِنَّ
   iii. يَنْصُرُ   vii. ذٰلِكَ
   iv.   يَضْرِبْنَ   viii. اِسْمَعِيْ

2. Translate the following sentences and identify the مَبْنِيٌّ and مُعْرَبٌ words in them.

   i.   نَظَرْتُ إِلَى الزَّهْرَةِ   v.   مَتَى يُسَافِرُ عَلِيٌّ؟
   ii.   أَخَذْتُ الْكِتَابَ مِنَ الصَّدِيقِ   vi.   أَلْأَبُ فِي الدَّارِ
   iii. فَرِحَ الطَّالِبُ بِالنَّتِيْجَةِ   vii. اَلْوَلَدُ مُؤَدَّبٌ
   iv.   كَيْفَ جَاءَ خَالِدٌ؟   viii. اَللهُ يُحِبُّ الْمُحْسِنِيْنَ

Section 2.4
أَقْسَامُ الْأَسْمَاءِ الْمَبْنِيَّةِ – Types of Indeclinable Nouns

The types of اَلْأَسْمَاءُ الْمَبْنِيَّةُ are as follows:

1. اَلضَّمَائِرُ (personal pronouns)
2. اَلْأَسْمَاءُ الْمَوْصُوْلَةُ (relative pronouns)
3. أَسْمَاءُ الْإِشَارَةِ (demonstrative pronouns)
4. أَسْمَاءُ الْأَفْعَالِ (those nouns which have the meaning of verbs)
5. أَسْمَاءُ الْأَصْوَاتِ (those nouns which denote a sound)
6. اَلظُّرُوْفُ (adverbs)
7. اَلْكِنَايَاتُ (those nouns which indicate an unspecified quantity)
8. اَلْمُرَكَّبُ الْبِنَائِيُّ (numerical phrase)

In the following pages, we will look at each of these in detail.

Section 2.4.1[16]
اَلضَّمَائِرُ – Personal Pronouns

We have discussed ضَمَائِرُ before. Now, we will look at them in greater detail.

Definition: ضَمَائِرُ (singular: ضَمِيرٌ) are those words, which are used in place of names and refer to the speaker (مُتَكَلِّمٌ) or the second person (حَاضِرٌ) or the third person (غَائِبٌ).

There are two types of ضَمَائِرُ:

1. اَلضَّمِيرُ الْبَارِزُ – Visible or Independent Pronoun: It is that ضَمِيرٌ, which is visible and has a distinct form. It can appear on its own, i.e. unattached to another word (known as مُنْفَصِلٌ), or it can be attached to another word (known as مُتَّصِلٌ). These two are defined as follows:

    i. اَلضَّمِيرُ الْمُنْفَصِلُ: The unattached pronoun is that pronoun which can be pronounced on its own without being connected to another word.

    ii. اَلضَّمِيرُ الْمُتَّصِلُ: The attached pronoun is that pronoun which cannot be pronounced on its own without being connected to another word.

2. اَلضَّمِيرُ الْمُسْتَتِرُ – Hidden or Implied Pronoun: It is that ضَمِيرٌ, which is not visible but is implied. It is always attached (مُتَّصِلٌ).

    <u>Note:</u> A hidden ضَمِيرٌ can only appear in حَالَةُ الرَّفْعِ. (refer to Table 2.2)

Below are tables showing different forms that the ضَمَائِرُ will assume in the various conditions/states (*haalaat*).

---

[16] For more details, examples, and exercises, please refer to *al-Nahw al-Wadih, Ibtida'iyyah*, vol. 2, 120-135.

Table 2.1
ضَمِيْرٌ مُنْفَصِلٌ (بَارِزٌ) ضَمِيْرٌ مُنْفَصِلٌ in حَالَةُ الرَّفْعِ (also called ضَمِيْرٌ مَرْفُوعٌ مُنْفَصِلٌ)

وَاحِدٌ مُذَكَّرٌ غَائِبٌ	هُوَ
تَثْنِيَةٌ مُذَكَّرٌ غَائِبٌ	هُمَا
جَمْعٌ مُذَكَّرٌ غَائِبٌ	هُمْ
وَاحِدٌ مُؤَنَّثٌ غَائِبٌ	هِيَ
تَثْنِيَةٌ مُؤَنَّثٌ غَائِبٌ	هُمَا
جَمْعٌ مُؤَنَّثٌ غَائِبٌ	هُنَّ
وَاحِدٌ مُذَكَّرٌ حَاضِرٌ	أَنْتَ
تَثْنِيَةٌ مُذَكَّرٌ حَاضِرٌ	أَنْتُمَا
جَمْعٌ مُذَكَّرٌ حَاضِرٌ	أَنْتُمْ
وَاحِدٌ مُؤَنَّثٌ حَاضِرٌ	أَنْتِ
تَثْنِيَةٌ مُؤَنَّثٌ حَاضِرٌ	أَنْتُمَا
جَمْعٌ مُؤَنَّثٌ حَاضِرٌ	أَنْتُنَّ
وَاحِدٌ مُتَكَلِّمٌ (مُذَكَّرٌ وَمُؤَنَّثٌ)	أَنَا
تَثْنِيَةٌ وَجَمْعٌ مُتَكَلِّمٌ (مُذَكَّرٌ وَمُؤَنَّثٌ)	نَحْنُ

e.g.   رَجُلٌ   هُوَ
       خَبَرٌ   مُبْتَدَأٌ
              (حَالَةُ الرَّفْعِ)

Table 2.2
(ضَمِيرٌ مَرْفُوعٌ مُتَّصِلٌ also called) حَالَةُ الرَّفْعِ in ضَمِيرٌ مُتَّصِلٌ

	بَارِزٌ		مُسْتَتِرٌ		
	—	—	يَضْرِبُ (هُوَ)	ضَرَبَ (هُوَ)	وَاحِدٌ مُذَكَّرٌ غَائِبٌ
	ضَرَبَا (ا)	يَضْرِبَانِ (ا)	—	—	تَثْنِيَةٌ مُذَكَّرٌ غَائِبٌ
	ضَرَبُوا (و)	يَضْرِبُونَ (و)	—	—	جَمْعٌ مُذَكَّرٌ غَائِبٌ
	—	—	تَضْرِبُ (هِيَ)	ضَرَبَتْ (هِيَ)	وَاحِدٌ مُؤَنَّثٌ غَائِبٌ
	ضَرَبَتَا (ا)	تَضْرِبَانِ (ا)	—	—	تَثْنِيَةٌ مُؤَنَّثٌ غَائِبٌ
	ضَرَبْنَ (ن)	يَضْرِبْنَ (ن)	—	—	جَمْعٌ مُؤَنَّثٌ غَائِبٌ
	ضَرَبْتَ (تَ)	—	تَضْرِبُ (أَنْتَ)	—	وَاحِدٌ مُذَكَّرٌ حَاضِرٌ
	ضَرَبْتُمَا (تُمَا)	تَضْرِبَانِ (ا)	—	—	تَثْنِيَةٌ مُذَكَّرٌ حَاضِرٌ
	ضَرَبْتُمْ (تُمْ)	تَضْرِبُونَ (و)	—	—	جَمْعٌ مُذَكَّرٌ حَاضِرٌ
	ضَرَبْتِ (تِ)	تَضْرِبِينَ (ي)	—	—	وَاحِدٌ مُؤَنَّثٌ حَاضِرٌ
	ضَرَبْتُمَا (تُمَا)	تَضْرِبَانِ (ا)	—	—	تَثْنِيَةٌ مُؤَنَّثٌ حَاضِرٌ
	ضَرَبْتُنَّ (تُنَّ)	تَضْرِبْنَ (ن)	—	—	جَمْعٌ مُؤَنَّثٌ حَاضِرٌ
	ضَرَبْتُ (تُ)	—	—	أَضْرِبُ (أَنَا)	وَاحِدٌ مُتَكَلِّمٌ (مُذَكَّرٌ وَمُؤَنَّثٌ)
	ضَرَبْنَا (نَا)	—	—	نَضْرِبُ (نَحْنُ)	تَثْنِيَةٌ وَجَمْعٌ مُتَكَلِّمٌ (مُذَكَّرٌ وَمُؤَنَّثٌ)

Note: In the table above, the ضَمِيرٌ مُتَّصِلٌ, which in many cases is the فَاعِلٌ, is indicated after its respective verb in parentheses.

Table 2.3

حَالَةُ النَّصْبِ in ضَمِيرٌ مُتَّصِلٌ and ضَمِيرٌ مُنْفَصِلٌ (also called ضَمِيرٌ مَنْصُوبٌ مُنْفَصِلٌ and ضَمِيرٌ مَنْصُوبٌ مُتَّصِلٌ)

	ضَمِيرٌ مَنْصُوبٌ مُتَّصِلٌ (بَارِزٌ)		ضَمِيرٌ مَنْصُوبٌ مُنْفَصِلٌ (بَارِزٌ)
	Example	Dameer	
وَاحِدٌ مُذَكَّرٌ غَائِبٌ	ضَرَبَهُ	هُ	إِيَّاهُ
تَثْنِيَةٌ مُذَكَّرٌ غَائِبٌ	ضَرَبَهُمَا	هما	إِيَّاهُمَا
جَمْعٌ مُذَكَّرٌ غَائِبٌ	ضَرَبَهُمْ	هم	إِيَّاهُمْ
وَاحِدٌ مُؤَنَّثٌ غَائِبٌ	ضَرَبَهَا	ها	إِيَّاهَا
تَثْنِيَةٌ مُؤَنَّثٌ غَائِبٌ	ضَرَبَهُمَا	ها	إِيَّاهُمَا
جَمْعٌ مُؤَنَّثٌ غَائِبٌ	ضَرَبَهُنَّ	هن	إِيَّاهُنَّ
وَاحِدٌ مُذَكَّرٌ حَاضِرٌ	ضَرَبَكَ	ك	إِيَّاكَ
تَثْنِيَةٌ مُذَكَّرٌ حَاضِرٌ	ضَرَبَكُمَا	كما	إِيَّاكُمَا
جَمْعٌ مُذَكَّرٌ حَاضِرٌ	ضَرَبَكُمْ	كم	إِيَّاكُمْ
وَاحِدٌ مُؤَنَّثٌ حَاضِرٌ	ضَرَبَكِ	ك	إِيَّاكِ
تَثْنِيَةٌ مُؤَنَّثٌ حَاضِرٌ	ضَرَبَكُمَا	كما	إِيَّاكُمَا
جَمْعٌ مُؤَنَّثٌ حَاضِرٌ	ضَرَبَكُنَّ	كن	إِيَّاكُنَّ
وَاحِدٌ مُتَكَلِّمٌ (مُذَكَّرٌ وَمُؤَنَّثٌ)	ضَرَبَنِي[17]	ي	إِيَّايَ
تَثْنِيَةٌ وَجَمْعٌ مُتَكَلِّمٌ (مُذَكَّرٌ وَمُؤَنَّثٌ)	ضَرَبَنَا	نا	إِيَّانَا

e.g.   نَعْبُدُ   إِيَّاكَ   You alone we worship.
      فِعْلٌ مَعَ فَاعِلِهِ   مَفْعُولٌ مُقَدَّمٌ (حَالَةُ النَّصْبِ)

---

[17] Sometimes, a ن (نُونُ الْوِقَايَةِ) is added before the يَاءُ ضَمِيرٌ to protect an *i'raab* as in ضَرَبَنِي, which would otherwise be incorrectly read as ضَرَبِي (the لَامُ كَلِمَةٍ of الْفِعْلُ الْمَاضِي is مَبْنِيٌّ عَلَى الْفَتْحِ).

There are two ways in which (بَارِزٌ) ضَمِيْرٌ مُتَّصِلٌ appears in حَالَةُ الجَرِّ. One is when it is preceded by a حَرْفُ جَرٍّ; and the other is when some other word is مُضَافٌ to it.

Table 2.4
حَالَةُ الجَرِّ in ضَمِيْرٌ مُتَّصِلٌ (بَارِزٌ) (also called ضَمِيْرٌ مَجْرُوْرٌ مُتَّصِلٌ)

بِحَرْفِ الجَرِّ	بِالإِضَافَةِ	
لَهُ	دَارُهُ	وَاحِدٌ مُذَكَّرٌ غَائِبٌ
لَهُمَا	دَارُهُمَا	تَثْنِيَةٌ مُذَكَّرٌ غَائِبٌ
لَهُمْ	دَارُهُمْ	جَمْعٌ مُذَكَّرٌ غَائِبٌ
لَهَا	دَارُهَا	وَاحِدٌ مُؤَنَّثٌ غَائِبٌ
لَهُمَا	دَارُهُمَا	تَثْنِيَةٌ مُؤَنَّثٌ غَائِبٌ
لَهُنَّ	دَارُهُنَّ	جَمْعٌ مُؤَنَّثٌ غَائِبٌ
لَكَ	دَارُكَ	وَاحِدٌ مُذَكَّرٌ حَاضِرٌ
لَكُمَا	دَارُكُمَا	تَثْنِيَةٌ مُذَكَّرٌ حَاضِرٌ
لَكُمْ	دَارُكُمْ	جَمْعٌ مُذَكَّرٌ حَاضِرٌ
لَكِ	دَارُكِ	وَاحِدٌ مُؤَنَّثٌ حَاضِرٌ
لَكُمَا	دَارُكُمَا	تَثْنِيَةٌ مُؤَنَّثٌ حَاضِرٌ
لَكُنَّ	دَارُكُنَّ	جَمْعٌ مُؤَنَّثٌ حَاضِرٌ
لِي	دَارِيْ	وَاحِدٌ مُتَكَلِّمٌ (مُذَكَّرٌ وَمُؤَنَّثٌ)
لَنَا	دَارُنَا	تَثْنِيَةٌ وَجَمْعٌ مُتَكَلِّمٌ (مُذَكَّرٌ وَمُؤَنَّثٌ)

e.g.   His house is his.   دَارُهُ   لَهُ

مُضَافٌ + مُضَافٌ إِلَيْهِ   حَرْفُ جَرٍّ + مَجْرُوْرٌ

(ضَمِيْرٌ مُتَّصِلٌ مَجْرُوْرٌ بِالإِضَافَةِ)   (ضَمِيْرٌ مُتَّصِلٌ مَجْرُوْرٌ بِحَرْفِ الجَرِّ)

Note: The ضَمِيْرٌ بَارِزٌ in حَالَةُ الجَرِّ will always be مُتَّصِلٌ.

ضَمِيْرُ الشَّأْنِ:

It is that ضَمِيْرٌ غَائِبٌ مُذَكَّرٌ, which sometimes appears at the beginning of a sentence without a مَرْجَعٌ (an earlier word that it refers to). The sentence after it clarifies such a ضَمِيْرٌ.

e.g. إِنَّهُ زَيْدٌ قَائِمٌ   Indeed, the matter is that Zayd is standing.

ضَمِيْرُ الْقِصَّةِ:

It is that ضَمِيْرٌ غَائِبٌ مُؤَنَّثٌ, which sometimes appears at the beginning of a sentence without a مَرْجَعٌ (an earlier word that it refers to). The sentence after it clarifies such a ضَمِيْرٌ.

e.g. إِنَّهَا فَاطِمَةُ قَائِمَةٌ   Indeed, the matter is that Fatimah is standing.

ضَمِيْرُ الْفَصْلِ:

It is that ضَمِيْرٌ, which appears between a مُبْتَدَأٌ and a خَبَرٌ for emphasis.

e.g. أُولَئِكَ هُمُ الْمُفْلِحُوْنَ   It is they who are successful.

EXERCISE

1. Translate, fill in the *i'raab* and analyze the following sentences, pointing out all the ضَمَائِرُ, as well as their type and حَالَاتٌ.

    i. القطار قدم في وقته   iii. نَصَرَنَا
    ii. نحن نرزقك   iv. الله يرزقها وإياكم

Section 2.4.2[18]
اَلْأَسْمَاءُ الْمَوْصُوْلَةُ - Relative Pronouns

Definition: An اِسْمٌ مَوْصُوْلٌ is an اِسْمٌ مَعْرِفَةٌ whose meaning/purpose is understood through the sentence, which comes after it, which is called صِلَةٌ.

- An اِسْمٌ مَوْصُوْلٌ cannot form a complete part of a sentence on its own. It must have a صِلَةٌ which relates (refers back) to it. The صِلَةٌ, which is generally a جُمْلَةٌ خَبَرِيَّةٌ, must have a ضَمِيْرٌ (visible or hidden) referring to the اِسْمٌ مَوْصُوْلٌ. This ضَمِيْرٌ is called عَائِدٌ.

Table 2.5
اَلْأَسْمَاءُ الْمَوْصُوْلَةُ لِلْمُذَكَّرِ

وَاحِدٌ	اَلَّذِيْ	who, that, which	
تَثْنِيَةٌ	اَللَّذَانِ	those two who, that, which	حَالَةُ الرَّفْعِ
تَثْنِيَةٌ	اَللَّذَيْنِ	those two who, that, which	حَالَةُ النَّصْبِ وَالْجَرِّ
جَمْعٌ	اَلَّذِيْنَ	those who, that, which	

Table 2.6
اَلْأَسْمَاءُ الْمَوْصُوْلَةُ لِلْمُؤَنَّثِ

وَاحِدٌ	اَلَّتِيْ	who, that, which	
تَثْنِيَةٌ	اَللَّتَانِ	those two who, that, which	حَالَةُ الرَّفْعِ
تَثْنِيَةٌ	اَللَّتَيْنِ	those two who, that, which	حَالَةُ النَّصْبِ وَالْجَرِّ
جَمْعٌ	اَللَّائِيْ	those who, that, which	
جَمْعٌ	اَللَّوَانِيْ	those who, that, which	

Examples

1. جَاءَ الَّذِيْ نَصَرَكَ — **The one** (masculine) who helped you, came.
2. جَاءَ اللَّذَانِ نَصَرَاكَ — **The two** (masculine) who helped you, came.
3. رَأَيْتُ اللَّذَيْنِ ضَرَبَاكَ — I saw **the two** (masculine) who hit you.
4. لَقِيْتُ الَّذِيْنَ نَصَرُوْنِيْ — I met **those** (masculine) who helped me.
5. جَاءَتِ الَّتِيْ نَصَرَتْكَ — **The one** (feminine) who helped you, came.
6. جَاءَتِ اللَّتَانِ نَصَرَتَاكَ — **The two** (feminine) who helped you, came.

---

[18] For more examples and exercises, please refer to *al-Nahw al-Wadih, Ibtida'iyyah*, vol. 2, 136-140.

	7.	رَأَيْتُ اللَّتَيْنِ ضَرَبَتَاكَ	I saw **the two** (feminine) who hit you.
	8.	جَاءَتِ اللَّائِيْ نَصَرْنَكَ	**Those** (feminine) who helped you, came.

Additional Relative Pronouns:

1. مَا and مَنْ (that and who)
   - These are used for all genders and all numbers.
   - The difference is that مَنْ is used for intelligent beings (ذَوِى الْعُقُوْلِ) and مَا is used for non-intelligent beings (غَيْرِ ذَوِى الْعُقُوْلِ).

   e.g. أَحْسِنْ اِلٰى مَنْ أَحْسَنَ إِلَيْكَ   Show goodness to that person who has shown goodness to you.

   قَرَأْتُ مَا كَتَبْتَ   I read what you wrote.

2. أَيٌّ and أَيَّةٌ
   - They are generally مُعْرَبٌ and used in إِضَافَةٌ.
   - أَيٌّ has the meaning of اَلَّذِيْ.

   e.g. مِنْ أَيِّ كِتَابٍ   from which book...

   - أَيَّةٌ has the meaning of اَلَّتِيْ.

   e.g. أَيَّةُ بِنْتٍ   which girl...

3. ال, which appears before an اِسْمُ فَاعِلٍ and an اِسْمُ مَفْعُوْلٍ, has the effect of اِسْمُ مَوْصُوْلٌ.

   e.g. اَلضَّارِبُ   would equal   اَلَّذِيْ ضَرَبَ
   اَلْمَضْرُوْبُ   would equal   اَلَّذِيْ ضُرِبَ
   اَلسَّامِعُوْنَ   would equal   اَلَّذِيْنَ سَمِعُوْا

4. ذُوْ

   According to the dialect of the tribe بَنُوْ طَيٍّ, it is an اِسْمُ مَوْصُوْلٌ.
   It is used for all genders and all numbers, without its form changing.

   e.g. جَاءَ ذُوْ ضَرَبَكَ   equals   جَاءَ الَّذِيْ ضَرَبَكَ   The one who hit you, came.
   رَأَيْتُ ذُوْ ضَرَبَكَ   equals   رَأَيْتُ الَّذِيْ ضَرَبَكَ   I saw the one who hit you.
   مَرَرْتُ بِذُوْ ضَرَبَكَ   equals   مَرَرْتُ بِالَّذِيْ ضَرَبَكَ   I passed by the one who hit you.

Sentence Analysis:

جَاءَ الَّذِيْ أَبُوْهُ عَالِمٌ That person whose father is knowledgeable, came.

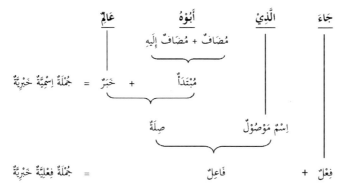

EXERCISE

1. Translate, fill in the *i'raab*, and analyze the following sentences.

   i. أين الذي ضرب زيدا؟

   ii. الله يعلم ما في الأرض

   iii. جاءت اللتان تسكنان أمامنا

   iv. إن الذين كفروا لا يدخلون الجنة

Section 2.4.3[19]
أَسْمَاءُ الْإِشَارَةِ – Demonstrative Pronouns

Definition: An إِسْمُ الْإِشَارَةِ is that noun, which is used to point at something. These nouns are of of two types.
  i. لِلْقَرِيْبِ: It is used for pointing at something near.
  ii. لِلْبَعِيْدِ: It is used for pointing at something far.

Table 2.7
أَسْمَاءُ الْإِشَارَةِ لِلْمُذَكَّرِ

	لِلْقَرِيْبِ			لِلْبَعِيْدِ		
وَاحِدٌ	هٰذَا	this		ذٰلِكَ	that	
تَثْنِيَةٌ	هٰذَانِ	these two...	حَالَةُ الرَّفْعِ	ذَانِكَ	those two...	حَالَةُ الرَّفْعِ
تَثْنِيَةٌ	هٰذَيْنِ	these two...	حَالَةُ النَّصْبِ وَالْجَرِّ	ذَيْنِكَ	those two...	حَالَةُ النَّصْبِ وَالْجَرِّ
جَمْعٌ	هٰؤُلَاءِ	these		أُولٰئِكَ	those	

Table 2.8
أَسْمَاءُ الْإِشَارَةِ لِلْمُؤَنَّثِ

	لِلْقَرِيْبِ			لِلْبَعِيْدِ		
وَاحِدٌ	هٰذِهِ	this		تِلْكَ	that	
تَثْنِيَةٌ	هَاتَانِ	these two...	حَالَةُ الرَّفْعِ	تَانِكَ	those two...	حَالَةُ الرَّفْعِ
تَثْنِيَةٌ	هَاتَيْنِ	these two...	حَالَةُ النَّصْبِ وَالْجَرِّ	تَيْنِكَ	those two...	حَالَةُ النَّصْبِ وَالْجَرِّ
جَمْعٌ	هٰؤُلَاءِ	these		أُولٰئِكَ	those	

e.g. ذٰلِكَ الْكِتَابُ   that book
      هٰؤُلَاءِ النِّسَاءُ   these women
      أُولٰئِكَ الرِّجَالُ   those men

---

[19] For more examples and exercises, please refer to *al-Nahw al-Wadih, Ibtida'iyyah*, vol. 2, 141-145.

Notes:

1. In the case of أَسْمَاءُ الْإِشَارَةِ لِلْقَرِيْبِ, for both masculine and feminine, the هـ in the beginning is not part of the actual اِسْمُ الْإِشَارَةِ. It is, in fact, a حَرْفُ تَنْبِيْهٍ. However, it is so often used with the أَسْمَاءُ الْإِشَارَةِ لِلْقَرِيْبِ, that it is normally considered a part of them.

2. The ك of اِسْمُ الْإِشَارَةِ (الْبَعِيْدُ) is sometimes changed according to the number of persons being addressed. The meaning will not be affected.

   e.g. ذٰلِكُمَا رَبُّكُمَا   He is the Lord of both of you.

3. If the مُشَارٌ إِلَيْهِ is a مُضَافٌ, then the اِسْمُ الْإِشَارَةِ will come after the مُضَافٌ إِلَيْهِ.

   e.g. كِتَابُكَ هٰذَا   this book of yours

4. If the اِسْمُ الْإِشَارَةِ occurs as a مُبْتَدَأٌ, then the خَبَرٌ will generally be a نَكِرَةٌ.

   e.g. هٰذَا كِتَابٌ   This is a book.

   However, if the خَبَرٌ is also مَعْرِفَةٌ, then a suitable ضَمِيْرٌ should be added between the مُبْتَدَأٌ, which is an اِسْمُ الْإِشَارَةِ, and the خَبَرٌ for it to remain a complete sentence.

   e.g. هٰذَا هُوَ الْكِتَابُ   This is the book.

   If no ضَمِيْرٌ is added, it would be an incomplete sentence.

   e.g. هٰذَا الْكِتَابُ   this book

5. If the خَبَرٌ is a مُضَافٌ, then there will be no need for a ضَمِيْرٌ to be added between the مُبْتَدَأٌ and the خَبَرٌ.

   e.g. هٰذَا اِبْنُ الْمَلِكِ   This is the son of the king.

6. هُنَا or هٰهُنَا (here) and هُنَاكَ (there) are also اِسْمُ الْإِشَارَةِ. However, they do not have any special rules.

Sentence Analysis:

This pen is precious.

EXERCISE

1. Translate, fill in the *i'raab*, and analyze the following sentences.

    i. تلك السيارة قديمة

    ii. أولئك تجار صادقون

    iii. هؤلاء طلاب المدرسة

    iv. هذه حجرة واسعة

    v. هذان ولدان مهذبان

    vi. هذان الولدان مهذبان

Section 2.4.4[20]
أَسْمَاءُ الْأَفْعَالِ – Those Nouns Which Have the Meaning of Verbs

Definition: These are nouns that have the meaning of verbs but do not accept its signs.

- That which has the meaning of الْفِعْلُ الْمَاضِي, gives the noun after it a *raf'*; and the one which has the meaning of الْأَمْرُ الْحَاضِرُ, gives the noun after it a *nasb*.

Table 2.9
Nouns in the Meaning of الْفِعْلُ الْمَاضِي

Noun	Verb	Meaning	Example	
هَيْهَاتَ	بَعُدَ	he/it became far, it is far (from him)	هَيْهَاتَ زَيْدٌ أَنْ يَفْعَلَ هٰذَا	It is far from (beyond) Zayd to do this.
شَتَّانَ	بَعُدَ وَ افْتَرَقَ	same as above; and what a difference, there is a difference between	شَتَّانَ بَيْنَ الْعَالِمِ وَالْجَاهِلِ	What a difference there is between the learned and the ignorant!
سَرْعَانَ	سَرُعَ	he hastened	سَرْعَانَ زَيْدٌ	Zayd hastened.

Table 2.10
Nouns in the Meaning of الْأَمْرُ الْحَاضِرُ

Noun	Verb	Meaning	Example	
رُوَيْدَ	أَمْهِلْ	Give respite!	رُوَيْدَ زَيْدًا	Give Zayd respite.
بَلْهَ	دَعْ	Leave!; Give up!	بَلْهَ التَّفَكُّرَ فِيمَا لَا يَعْنِيكَ	Give up thinking about that which does not concern you.
دُونَكَ – هَا	خُذْ	Take!	دُونَكَ اللَّبَنَ	Take the milk.
عَلَيْكَ	الْزَمْ	Hold on to (it)!; (It is) incumbent on you	عَلَيْكَ بِسُنَّتِي	Hold on to my Sunnah.
حَيَّهَلْ – حَيَّ هَيْتَ – هَلُمَّ	ائْتِ – عَجِّلْ أَقْبِلْ	Come!; Hasten!	حَيَّ عَلَى الصَّلَاةِ	Come to *salah*.

---

[20] For more examples and exercises, please refer to 'Ali al-Jaarim & Mustafa Ameen, *al-Nahw al-Wadih li al-Madaris al-Thanawiyyah*, (Cairo: Dar al-Ma'arif, n.d.), vol. 1, 40-43.

Notes:

1. There are some other nouns which have the meaning of verbs. These are as follows:

    (اِسْتَجِبْ) أَمِيْنْ – accept)   (اِنْتِ) تَعَالَ – come)

    (اِكْتَفِ) فَقَطْ – suffice)   (اُسْكُتْ) صَهْ – keep quite)

    (تَبَعَّدْ عَنِّيْ) إِلَيْكَ عَنِّيْ – away from me)   (اِعْطِ) هَاتِ – bring, give)

    (جِئْ بِهِ عِنْدِيْ) عَلَيَّ بِهِ – bring him/it to me)

2. Some of these nouns are inflectable (مُتَصَرِّفٌ), i.e. their form changes.

    i. هَاتِ هَاتِيَا هَاتُوا هَاتِي هَاتِيَا هَاتِيْنَ

    e.g. قُلْ هَاتُوا بُرْهَنَكُمْ إِنْ كُنْتُمْ صٰدِقِيْنَ

    Say: bring your proof, if you are truthful.

    ii. تَعَالَ تَعَالَيَا تَعَالَوْا تَعَالَيْ تَعَالَيَا تَعَالَيْنَ

    e.g. قُلْ يَأَهْلَ الْكِتٰبِ تَعَالَوْا إِلَىٰ كَلِمَةٍ...الآية[21]

    Say: O people of the book! Come to a word...

    e.g. فَتَعَالَيْنَ أُمَتِّعْكُنَّ وَ أُسَرِّحْكُنَّ سَرَاحًا جَمِيْلًا (القرآن)

    Then, come, I will make provision for you and release you with kindness.

Section 2.4.5
أَسْمَاءُ الأَصْوَاتِ – Those Nouns Which Denote a Sound

أَخْ أَخْ	To denote a cough.
أُفْ	To denote pain.
بَخْ	To denote happiness, pleasure.
نَخَّ	To make a camel sit.
غَاقَ	To denote the cawing of a crow.

---

[21] الآية is an abbreviation for إِلَىٰ آخِرِ الْآيَةِ (until the end of the *ayah*).

Section 2.4.6[22]
اَلظُّرُوفُ – Adverbs

Definition: An ظَرْفٌ اِسْمُ is that noun, which gives us an idea of the place or time when (or where) some work is done. It is also called مَفْعُولٌ فِيهِ.

ظُرُوفٌ are of two kinds: ظَرْفُ الزَّمَانِ (adverb of time) and ظَرْفُ الْمَكَانِ (the adverb of place).

ظُرُوفُ الزَّمَانِ – Adverbs of Time:

1. إِذْ   (when)
   - It gives the meaning of فِعْلٌ مُاضِي even when it appears before فِعْلٌ مُضَارِعٌ.
   - The sentence after إِذْ could be a جُمْلَةٌ اِسْمِيَّةٌ or a جُمْلَةٌ فِعْلِيَّةٌ.
     - e.g. وَاذْكُرُوا إِذْ أَنْتُمْ قَلِيلٌ   Remember when you were less.
     - e.g. وَإِذْ يَرْفَعُ إِبْرَاهِيمُ الْقَوَاعِدَ مِنَ الْبَيْتِ   And when Ibrahim (Allah give him peace) was raising the foundation of the House (Ka'ba).
   - Sometimes, it gives the meaning of suddenness (مُفَاجَأَةٌ). This is called إِذْ الْفُجَائِيَّةُ.
     - e.g. خَرَجْتُ إِذْ مُدِيرُ الْمَدْرَسَةِ نَاظِرٌ   I came out and suddenly the principal of the school was watching.
   - Sometimes, it gives the meaning of because (لِأَنَّ). This is called إِذْ التَّعْلِيلِيَّةُ.
     - e.g. لَنْ يَنْفَعَكُمُ الْيَوْمَ إِذْ ظَلَمْتُمْ أَنَّكُمْ فِي الْعَذَابِ مُشْتَرِكُونَ (القرآن)
       That you are together in punishment will never benefit you today because you oppressed.
       [This is according to one translation.]

2. إِذَا   (when/if)
   - It gives the meaning of فِعْلٌ مُضَارِعٌ even when it appears before فِعْلٌ مَاضِي.
   - It gives the meaning of شَرْطٌ and جَزَاءٌ but does not give either a جَزْمٌ.
   - The sentence after إِذَا could be a جُمْلَةٌ اِسْمِيَّةٌ or preferably a جُمْلَةٌ فِعْلِيَّةٌ.
     - e.g. أَتِيكَ إِذَا الشَّمْسُ طَالِعَةٌ   I will come to you when the sun is up.
     - e.g. إِذَا جَاءَ نَصْرُ اللهِ... الآية   When the help of Allah comes...

---

[22] The list of ظُرُوفٌ given in this section is by no means exhaustive. There are many more that should be studied in advanced books of *Nahw*.

- Sometimes, it gives the meaning of suddenness (مُفَاجَأَةٌ), in which case إِذَا must be followed by a جُمْلَةٌ اِسْمِيَّةٌ.

  e.g. خَرَجْتُ فَإِذَا الْكَلْبُ وَاقِفٌ   I came out and suddenly the dog was standing.

3. مَتَى (when)
   - It can be used as an interrogative (اِسْتِفْهَامٌ).

     e.g. مَتَى تُسَافِرُ؟   When will you travel?
   - It can also be used as a conditional noun in which case the شَرْطٌ and جَزَاءٌ get a جَزْمٌ.

     e.g. مَتَى تَصُمْ أَصُمْ   When you fast, I will fast.

4. كَيْفَ (how)
   - It is used to enquire condition.

     e.g. كَيْفَ حَالُكَ؟   How are you? (In what condition are you?)

5. أَيَّانَ (when)
   - It is used as an interrogative.

     e.g. أَيَّانَ يَوْمُ الدِّيْنِ؟   When will be the day of recompense?

   Note: أَيَّانَ is used only to enquire of great events of the future as compared to مَتَى.

6. أَمْسِ (yesterday)

   e.g. جَاءَنِيْ زَيْدٌ أَمْسِ   Zayd came to me yesterday.

7. مُذْ – مُنْذُ (since, from)
   - These two can be used to convey the beginning of a time period.

     e.g. مَا رَأَيْتُهُ مُنْذُ/مُذْ يَوْمِ الْجُمُعَةِ   I have not seen him since Friday.
   - They can also be used to refer to an entire period.

     e.g. مَا رَأَيْتُهُ مُنْذُ/مُذْ يَوْمَيْنِ   I have not seen him for two days.
   - These can be used as حَرْفُ جَرٍّ (followed by a مَجْرُورٌ) **or** as اِسْمٌ, which will be regarded as a مُبْتَدَأٌ followed by a مَرْفُوعٌ.

     e.g. مَا رَأَيْتُهُ مُنْذُ/مُذْ يَوْمِ الْجُمُعَةِ   I have not seen him since Friday.

     مَا رَأَيْتُهُ مُنْذُ/مُذْ يَوْمُ الْجُمُعَةِ

8. قَطُّ   (not, never)
   - It is used to emphasize اَلْمَاضِيْ الْمَنْفِيُّ.
     - e.g.   مَا ضَرَبْتُهُ قَطُّ   I never hit him.

9. عَوْضُ   (never)
   - It is used to emphasize اَلْمُضَارِعُ الْمَنْفِيُّ.
     - e.g.   لَا أَضْرِبُهُ عَوْضُ   I will never hit him.

10. قَبْلُ   (before)
    بَعْدُ   (after)
    - They are مَبْنِيٌّ when they are مُضَافٌ and the مُضَافٌ إِلَيْهِ is not mentioned, but intended.
      - e.g.   لِلّٰهِ الْأَمْرُ مِنْ قَبْلُ وَ مِنْ بَعْدُ (أَيْ مِنْ قَبْلِ كُلِّ شَيْءٍ وَ مِنْ بَعْدِ كُلِّ شَيْءٍ)
        Allah's is the decision before and after (i.e. before everything and after everything).
      - e.g.   أَنَا حَاضِرٌ مِنْ قَبْلُ (أَيْ مِنْ قَبْلِكَ)
        I have been present from before (i.e. before you).
      - e.g.   مَتَى تَجِيْئُنَا بَعْدُ؟ (أَيْ بَعْدَ هٰذَا)
        When will you come after (i.e. after this)?
    - When the مُضَافٌ إِلَيْهِ is mentioned, they will be مُعْرَبٌ.
      - e.g.   مِنْ قَبْلِ الْفَتْحِ   before the victory

ظُرُوْفُ الْمَكَانِ – Adverbs of Place:

1. حَيْثُ   (where)
   - It is generally مُضَافٌ to a sentence.
     - e.g.   اِجْلِسْ حَيْثُ زَيْدٌ جَالِسٌ   Sit where Zayd is sitting.

2. قُدَّامُ   (in front of)   &   خَلْفُ   (behind)
   - It has the same rules as those for قَبْلُ and بَعْدُ.
     - e.g.   قَامَ النَّاسُ قُدَّامُ وَخَلْفُ (أَيْ قُدَّامَهُ وَخَلْفَهُ)
       The people stood in front and behind.
       (i.e. in front of him and behind him).

3. تَحْتُ (under) & فَوْقُ (on top, above)

- It has the same rules as those for قَبْلُ and بَعْدُ.

    e.g. (جَلَسَ زَيْدٌ تَحْتُ وَعَمْرٌو فَوْقُ (أَيْ تَحْتَ الشَّجَرَةِ وَ فَوْقَ الشَّجَرَةِ

    Zayd sat under and 'Amr above. (i.e. under the tree and above the tree.)

4. عِنْدَ (by, at, near, with)

    e.g. اَلْمَالُ عِنْدَ زَيْدٍ   The money is with Zayd.

    <u>Note:</u> عِنْدَ will get a *kasrah* if it is preceded by مِنْ.

    e.g. مِنْ عِنْدِ اللهِ   from Allah

5. أَيْنَ/أَنَّى (where)

- They are used for اِسْتِفْهَامٌ.

    e.g. أَيْنَ تَذْهَبُ – أَنَّى تَذْهَبُ؟ Where are you going?

- They are used for شَرْطٌ and شَرْطٌ and جَزَاءٌ will get a (جَزْمٌ).

    e.g. أَيْنَ تَجْلِسْ أَجْلِسْ   Where you sit, I will sit.

    أَنَّى تَجْلِسْ أَجْلِسْ

6. لَدَى/لَدُنْ (at, by, near, with (same meaning as عِنْدَ)).

    e.g. اَلْمَالُ لَدَى زَيْدٍ   The money is with Zayd.

    مِنْ لَدُنْ حَكِيْمٍ خَبِيْرٍ   from the All-Wise, All-Knowing

- لَدُنْ is generally preceded by مِنْ.
- When used in the meaning of possession (with), the difference between لَدَى/لَدُنْ and عِنْدَ is that in the case of لَدُنْ/لَدَى, the possessed thing must be present with the person; whereas, in the case of عِنْدَ, the possessed thing need not be present with the person.

<u>Note:</u> That adverb which is مُعْرَبٌ and is مُضَافٌ to a sentence or the word إِذْ, could be مَبْنِيٌّ عَلَى الْفَتْحِ <u>or</u> it could get the *i'raab* according to the عَامِلٌ.

e.g. the adverb يوم which is مُضَافٌ in the following *ayahs*:

هذَا يَوْمُ يَنْفَعُ الصَّادِقِيْنَ صِدْقُهُمْ and هذَا يَوْمَ يَنْفَعُ الصَّادِقِيْنَ صِدْقُهُمْ

This is the day when the truth of the truthful will benefit them.

وُجُوْهٌ يَوْمَئِذٍ and وُجُوْهٌ يَوْمَئِذٍ

faces on that day

EXERCISE

1. Translate the follows *ayahs* of the Qur'an and identify the ظُرُوفٌ in them. Also identify whether they are from among ظُرُوفُ الزَّمَانِ or ظُرُوفُ الْمَكَانِ.

i. يَوْمَ يَكُونُ النَّاسُ كَالْفَرَاشِ الْمَبْثُوثِ

ii. وَمَا جَعَلْنَا لِبَشَرٍ مِنْ قَبْلِكَ الْخُلْدَ

iii. فَسُبْحَانَ اللهِ حِينَ تُمْسُونَ وَحِينَ تُصْبِحُونَ

iv. قَالَ فَإِنَّا قَدْ فَتَنَّا قَوْمَكَ مِنْ بَعْدِكَ

v. إِذْ جَاءُوكُمْ مِنْ فَوْقِكُمْ

vi. مَا عِنْدِي مَا تَسْتَعْجِلُونَ بِهِ

vii. وَعَلَّمْنَاهُ مِنْ لَدُنَّا عِلْماً

viii. يَعْلَمُ مَا بَيْنَ أَيْدِيهِمْ وَمَا خَلْفَهُمْ

ix. إِذْ يَقُولُ لِصَاحِبِهِ لَا تَحْزَنْ إِنَّ اللهَ مَعَنَا

x. أَعَدَّ اللهُ لَهُمْ جَنَّاتٍ تَجْرِي مِنْ تَحْتِهَا الْأَنْهَارُ

Section 2.4.7
اَلْكِنَايَاتُ – Those Nouns Which Indicate an Unspecified Quantity

1. كَمْ، كَذَا (so many, so much, how many, how much)
   - They can be used for numbers
     - e.g. كَمْ دِرْهَمًا عِنْدَكَ؟ How many silver coins do you have?
     - e.g. أَخَذْتُ كَذَا دِرْهَمًا   I took this many silver coins.
   - كَذَا is also used in the meaning of "such and such."
     - e.g. قَالَ لِيْ كَذَا وَ كَذَا   He said to me such and such.

2. كَيْتَ، ذَيْتَ (so and so, such and such)
   - e.g. قُلْتُ كَيْتَ وَذَيْتَ or قُلْتُ كَيْتَ ذَيْتَ   I said such and such.
   - e.g. فَعَلْتُ كَيْتَ وَذَيْتَ or فَعَلْتُ كَيْتَ ذَيْتَ   I did such and such.

Section 2.4.8
اَلْمُرَكَّبُ الْبِنَائِيُّ – Numerical Phrase

This has been discussed earlier. Please, refer to section 1.4.3.

Section 2.5

أَقْسَامُ اَلْأَسْمَاءِ الْمُعْرَبَةِ – Types of Declinable Nouns

These are of two types:

1. مُنْصَرِفٌ

<u>Definition</u>: It is that noun which does **not** have two causes from amongst the nine causes that prevent declension (أَسْبَابُ مَنْعِ الصَّرْفِ) **or** one such cause, which is equivalent to two.

- It accepts all *harakaat* as well as *tanween*.

2. غَيْرُ مُنْصَرِفٍ

<u>Definition</u>: It is that noun which has two causes from amongst the nine causes that prevent declension (أَسْبَابُ مَنْعِ الصَّرْفِ) **or** one such cause, which is equivalent to two.

- Such a noun does not accept a *kasrah* and never gets a *tanween*. In حَالَةُ الْجَرِّ, it gets a *fathah* in place of a *kasrah*.

أَسْبَابُ مَنْعِ الصَّرْفِ [23]

There are nine reasons/causes which prevent *i'raab* changes. Each one of these has its own conditions, which must exist for it to be a cause. The nine causes are as follows:

1. عَدْلٌ	2. وَصْفٌ	3. عَلَمٌ	4. تَأْنِيثٌ	5. عُجْمَةٌ
6. تَرْكِيبٌ	7. أَلِفٌ وَنُونٌ زَائِدَتَانِ	8. وَزْنُ فِعْلٍ	9. جَمْعُ مُنْتَهَى الْجُمُوعِ	

1. عَدْلٌ: It refers to the case when a noun gives up its original form to assume a new form.

   عَدْلٌ is of two types:

   i. عَدْلٌ تَحْقِيقِيٌّ: It refers to the case when a noun has an original.

      e.g.   In the case of ثُلَاثَ (three and three together), the original is ثَلَاثَةٌ وَثَلَاثَةٌ.

   ii. عَدْلٌ تَقْدِيرِيٌّ: It refers to the case when it is assumed that a noun had an original because it is used as غَيْرُ مُنْصَرِفٍ by the Arabs.

      e.g.   The Arabs use عُمَرُ as غَيْرُ مُنْصَرِفٍ. However, there is only one apparent cause, عَلَمٌ. Therefore, in order to keep the grammar rule intact, it is assumed that the second reason is عَدْلٌ, and the original for عُمَرُ is عَامِرٌ.

---

[23] This discussion is based upon *Hidayat al-Nahw*. It is presented in an entirely different manner in *al-Nahw al-Wadih*. See *al-Nahw al-Wadih, Ibdtida'iyyah*, vol. 3, 125-133.

2. صِفَةٌ/وَصْفٌ: There can be two cases when a noun, which is a صِفَةٌ, would be *ghayr munsarif*.[24] These are as follows:

   i. The صِفَةٌ was originally devised to give a descriptive (وَصْفِيٌّ) meaning. If such a صِفَةٌ is on the *wazn* of (أَفْعَل), and does not accept *taa* for its مُؤَنَّثٌ, it will be *ghayr munsarif*.

   e.g. أَحْمَرُ   red   أَخْضَرُ   green

   ii. The صِفَةٌ has أَلِفٌ وَ نُوْنٌ زَائِدَتَانِ. Its conditions are given below in (7).

3. عَلَمٌ: It refers to the case when a noun is a proper noun (name of a person, place or thing).

   e.g. فَاطِمَةُ   female name

         حَضَرَمَوْتُ   name of a region in Yemen

4. تَأْنِيْثٌ: It refers to the case when a noun is such a feminine proper noun, which has one of the following characteristics:

   i. It ends with a round ة. For example, مَكَّةُ   طَلْحَةُ[25]

   ii. It does not end with a round ة and has more then three letters. For example, زَيْنَبُ.

   iii. It is a non-Arabic three-letter word and the middle letter is سَاكِنٌ. For example, مِصْرُ.

   Note:

   - All nouns ending in اَلْأَلِفُ الْمَقْصُوْرَةُ (ى) or اَلْأَلِفُ الْمَمْدُوْدَةُ (اء) are feminine.

     e.g. حُبْلَى   pregnant

           حَمْرَاءُ   red

   - Presence of اَلْأَلِفُ الْمَمْدُوْدَةُ (اء) or اَلْأَلِفُ الْمَقْصُوْرَةُ (ى) is **equivalent to two reasons**.

5. عُجْمَةٌ: It refers to the case when a word, which is a proper noun in a non-Arabic language, has either

   - more than three letters   e.g. إِبْرَاهِيْمُ

     or

   - has three letters and the middle letter is مُتَحَرِّكٌ.   e.g. شَتَرُ (name of a fort)

     - Thus, نُوْحٌ is *munsarif* because its middle letter is not مُتَحَرِّكٌ.

---

[24] *Sharh ibn 'Aqil*, vol. 3, 322-324.

[25] Even though طَلْحَة is a masculine proper noun, it is considered a feminine noun because of the presence of a round ة. For more discussion on the subject, see Section 3.4.

Note: The difference between نُوحٌ and مِصْرُ is that مِصْرُ is a feminine noun because of it being the name of a country, while نُوحٌ is not a feminine noun. Thus, مِصْرُ is *ghayr munsarif* because of تَأْنِيثٌ and عَلَمٌ, while نُوحٌ is *munsarif* because it only has عَلَمٌ. عُجْمَةٌ does not apply to either.

6. <u>تَرْكِيبٌ</u>: It refers to the case when a word is a combination of two words. This word must be an عَلَمٌ.

   e.g.   بَعْلَبَكُّ   name of a city in Lebanon

          حَضْرَمَوْتُ   name of a region in Yemen

7. <u>أَلِفٌ وَنُونٌ زَائِدَتَانِ</u>: It refers to the case when a noun ends with an أَلِفٌ and نُونٌ (ـَانِ) and one of the following is true:

   i. The أَلِفٌ and نُونٌ appear at the end of such a noun which is an عَلَمٌ (proper noun).

      e.g.   عُثْمَانُ   عِمْرَانُ

      Note: Thus, the word سَعْدَانٌ (grass) is not *ghayr munsarif* because it is not a proper noun.

   ii. The أَلِفٌ and نُونٌ appear at the end of such a صِفَةٌ whose feminine is **not** on the وَزْنٌ of فَعْلَانَةٌ.

       e.g.   سَكْرَانُ[26] intoxicated   عَطْشَانُ[27] thirsty

       Their feminines are **not** on the وَزْنٌ of فَعْلَانَةٌ.

       Note: Thus, the word نَدْمَانٌ is not *ghayr munsarif* because its feminine (نَدْمَانَةٌ) is on the *wazn* of فَعْلَانَةٌ.

- If the أَلِفٌ and نُونٌ are not extra or added (i.e. not زَائِدَتَانِ) but are part of the original letters of the word, then it will not be *ghayr munsarif*. For example, شَيْطَانٌ.

---

[26] سَكْرَانُ is mainly used as *ghayr munsarif* (without *tanween*), and is sometimes used as *munsarif* (with *tanween*). The reason is that it has two feminines. The main feminine is سَكْرَى, which requires that the masculine be *ghayr munsarif* (سَكْرَانُ). However, in the dialect of Banu Asad, the feminine is سَكْرَانَةٌ. This requires that the masculine be *munsarif* (سَكْرَانٌ). See E. W. Lane, *An Arabic-English Lexicon*, (Beirut: Librairie du Liban, 1968), book I, part 4, 1391.

[27] عَطْشَانُ is interchangeably used as *munsarif* (with *tanween*) and *ghayr munsarif* (without *tanween*). The reason is that it has two feminines. One is عَطْشَى, and the other is عَطْشَانَةٌ. Considering the first, it becomes *ghayr munsarif* (عَطْشَانُ); and considering the second, it becomes *munsarif* (عَطْشَانٌ). See Lane, book I, part 5, 2079.

8. وَزْنُ فِعْلٍ: It refers to the case when a proper noun (عَلَمٌ) is on the *wazn* of a فِعْلٌ or when a صِفَةٌ is on the *wazn* of أَفْعَلُ.

  e.g.   لَسْتَ بِأَسْبَقَ مِنْ أَحْمَدَ   You are not more advanced/ahead than Ahmad.

  Here, أَحْمَدُ is an عَلَمٌ and is on the *wazn* of the verb أَفْعَلُ, and أَسْبَقُ is a صِفَةٌ and is on the *wazn* of the verb أَفْعَلُ. Therefore, these two are *ghayr munsarif*.

  e.g.   جَاءَ يَزِيدُ   Yazeed came.

  Here, يَزِيدُ is an عَلَمٌ and is on the *wazn* of the verb يَفْعَلُ.

9. جَمْعُ مُنْتَهَى الجُمُوعِ: It is that plural, which has after the أَلِفُ الجَمْعِ (*alif* of plural) one of the following:

 i. two مُتَحَرِّكٌ letters. e.g. مَسَاجِدُ mosques
 ii. one مُشَدَّدٌ letter. e.g. دَوَابُّ animals
 iii. three letters, the middle letter being سَاكِنٌ. e.g. مَفَاتِيحُ keys

Note:

- If any of the above words ends with a round ة, it will not be *ghayr munsarif*.

  e.g.   صَيَاقِلَةٌ   polishers

- جَمْعُ مُنْتَهَى الجُمُوعِ is **equivalent to two reasons/causes**.

<u>General Note:</u> A *ghayr munsarif* noun **will** get a *kasrah* in حَالَةُ الجَرِّ in the following cases:

- when it is مُضَافٌ.   e.g.   صَلَّيْتُ فِي مَسَاجِدِهِمْ   I prayed in their mosques.
- when it has ال before it.   e.g.   ذَهَبْتُ إِلَى الْمَقَابِرِ   I went to the graves.

EXERCISES

1. Mention with reason why the following words are *munsarif* or *ghayr munsarif*.

 i. زُفَر [28] v. صحراء
 ii. شيطان vi. مصابيح
 iii. أسود vii. يزيد
 iv. أساتذة viii. غضبان [29]

---

[28] This is the name of a major Hanafi Imam. It is non-Arabic in origin and is pronounced with a *dammah* on the first letter and a *fathah* on the second letter.

[29] Its main feminine is غَضْبَى. In the dialect of Banu Asad, its feminine is غَضْبَانَةُ. See Lane, book I, part 6, 2265.

2. Translate, fill in the *i'raab* and point out with reason the words which are *ghayr munsarif*.

   i. مررت بعمر
   ii. ذهب أحمد مع زينب إلى مكة
   iii. لا تسئلوا عن أشياء...الآية
   iv. سقيت ولدا عطشان
   v. يا أهل يثرب...الآية
   vi. مررت بمساجد
   vii. شهر رمضان الذى أنزل فيه القرآن...الآية
   viii. إن الله اصطفى أدم ونوحا وأل إبراهيم وأل عمران على العلمين (القرآن)

Section 2.6
إِعْرَابُ أَقْسَامِ الْأَسْمَاءِ الْمُعْرَبَاتِ – *I'raab* of the Various Types of *Mu'rab* Nouns

We begin this section by defining some terms. Then, we will outline the *i'raab* of each of the various types of *mu'rab* nouns.

اَلْاِسْمُ الصَّحِيْحُ: It is that noun, which does not end with any of the حُرُوْفُ الْعِلَّةِ (و – ا – ي).

e.g. رَجُلٌ   man

اَلْاِسْمُ الْقَائِمُ مَقَامَ الصَّحِيْحِ: It is that noun, which ends with a و or ي preceded by a سُكُوْنٌ.

e.g. دَلْوٌ   bucket   ظَبْيٌ   deer

اَلْأَسْمَاءُ السِّتَّةُ الْمُكَبَّرَةُ: These are six nouns, which are not in their diminutive form (مُصَغَّرٌ). These are as follows:

أَبٌ	father	فَمٌ	mouth
أَخٌ	brother	هَنٌ	something insignificant
حَمٌ	brother-in-law	ذُو (plural: أُولُوْ)	someone who possesses something

اَلْاِسْمُ الْمَقْصُوْرُ: It is that noun, which ends with an اَلْأَلِفُ الْمَقْصُوْرَةُ (ى).

e.g. مُوْسَى

اَلْاِسْمُ الْمَنْقُوْصُ: It is that noun which ends with a ي preceded by a *kasrah*.

e.g. اَلْقَاضِيْ   the judge

Note: It should be remembered that the ي is visible in an اِسْمٌ مَنْقُوْصٌ when it is مَعْرِفَةٌ. When it is نَكِرَةٌ, the ي is not visible, e.g. اَلْقَاضِيْ becomes قَاضٍ. However, in حَالَةُ النَّصْبِ, it does become visible, e.g. رَأَيْتُ قَاضِيًا (I saw a judge).

Before we list the *i'raab* of each of the various types of *mu'rab* nouns in a table, it would be useful to remember that a simple method of illustrating different *i'raab* is to make three sentences on the following pattern:

حَالَةُ الْجَرِّ	حَالَةُ النَّصْبِ	حَالَةُ الرَّفْعِ
مَرَرْتُ بِزَيْدٍ	رَأَيْتُ زَيْدًا	جَاءَ زَيْدٌ
I passed by Zayd.	I saw Zayd.	Zayd came.

In these three sentences, the word زَيْدٌ is displaying the different *i'raab* according to the changing state (حَالَةٌ). Thus, it has a *dammah* in حَالَةُ الرَّفْعِ, and a *fathah* in حَالَةُ النَّصْبِ, and a *kasrah* in حَالَةُ الْجَرِّ.

Table 2.11
إِعْرَابُ أَقْسَامِ الْأَسْمَاءِ الْمُعْرَبَاتِ

Noun Type	حَالَةُ الرَّفْعِ	حَالَةُ النَّصْبِ	حَالَةُ الْجَرِّ	Examples for Each State		
اَلْمُفْرَدُ الْمُنْصَرِفُ الصَّحِيحُ	ضَمَّةٌ	فَتْحَةٌ	كَسْرَةٌ	مَرَرْتُ بِزَيْدٍ	رَأَيْتُ زَيْدًا	جَاءَ زَيْدٌ
اَلْمُفْرَدُ الْقَائِمُ مَقَامَ الصَّحِيحِ	ضَمَّةٌ	فَتْحَةٌ	كَسْرَةٌ	مَرَرْتُ بِظَبْيٍ	رَأَيْتُ ظَبْيًا	هٰذَا ظَبْيٌ
اَلْجَمْعُ الْمُكَسَّرُ الْمُنْصَرِفُ	ضَمَّةٌ	فَتْحَةٌ	كَسْرَةٌ	قُلْتُ لِرِجَالٍ[30]	رَأَيْتُ رِجَالًا	هُمْ رِجَالٌ
غَيْرُ الْمُنْصَرِفِ	ضَمَّةٌ	فَتْحَةٌ	فَتْحَةٌ	مَرَرْتُ بِعُمَرَ	رَأَيْتُ عُمَرَ	جَاءَ عُمَرُ
اَلْأَسْمَاءُ السِّتَّةُ الْمُكَبَّرَةُ a. When مُضَافٌ to any noun besides the ي dameer.[31]	و	ا	ي	مَرَرْتُ بِأَبِيْكَ	رَأَيْتُ أَبَاكَ	جَاءَ أَبُوْكَ
b. When مُضَافٌ to the ي dameer.	hidden	hidden	hidden	مَرَرْتُ بِأَبِيْ	رَأَيْتُ أَبِيْ	جَاءَ أَبِيْ
c. when not مُضَافٌ	ضَمَّةٌ	فَتْحَةٌ	كَسْرَةٌ	مَرَرْتُ بِأَبٍ	رَأَيْتُ أَبًا	جَاءَ أَبٌ
اَلْمُضَافُ إِلَى يَاءِ الْمُتَكَلِّمِ	hidden	hidden	hidden	مَرَرْتُ بِزَمِيْلِيْ	رَأَيْتُ زَمِيْلِيْ	جَاءَ زَمِيْلِيْ
اَلِاسْمُ الْمَقْصُورُ	hidden	hidden	hidden	مَرَرْتُ بِمُوسَى	رَأَيْتُ مُوسَى	جَاءَ مُوسَى
اَلِاسْمُ الْمَنْقُوصُ — مَعْرِفَةٌ	hidden	فَتْحَةٌ	hidden	مَرَرْتُ بِالْقَاضِيْ	رَأَيْتُ الْقَاضِيَ	جَاءَ الْقَاضِيْ
اَلِاسْمُ الْمَنْقُوصُ — نَكِرَةٌ	hidden	فَتْحَةٌ	hidden	مَرَرْتُ بِقَاضٍ	رَأَيْتُ قَاضِيًا	جَاءَ قَاضٍ
اَلْمُثَنَّى	ـَانِ	ـَيْنِ	ـَيْنِ	مَرَرْتُ بِرَجُلَيْنِ	رَأَيْتُ رَجُلَيْنِ	جَاءَ رَجُلَانِ
اِثْنَانِ (masculine) / اِثْنَتَانِ (feminine)	ـَانِ	ـَيْنِ	ـَيْنِ	مَرَرْتُ بِاثْنَتَيْنِ	رَأَيْتُ اثْنَتَيْنِ	جَاءَ اثْنَانِ
كِلَا (masculine) / كِلْتَا (feminine) (مُضَافٌ إِلَى الضَّمِيْرِ)	ـَا	ـَيْ	ـَيْ	مَرَرْتُ بِكِلَيْهِمَا	رَأَيْتُ كِلَيْهِمَا	جَاءَ كِلَاهُمَا[32]

---

[30] I said to some men.

[31] The م of فَمٌ is dropped when it is مُضَافٌ to any noun besides the ي dameer. For example, it is dropped in the followng hadith: ... (مَا تَجْعَلُ فِي فِي امْرَأَتِكَ) (Whatever you put in the mouth of your wife...)

[32] Both of them.

Table 2.11 – *Continued*

Noun Type	حَالَةُ الرَّفْعِ	حَالَةُ النَّصْبِ	حَالَةُ الْجَرِّ	Examples for Each State		
جَمْعُ الْمُؤَنَّثِ السَّالِمُ	ـَاتٌ	ـَاتٍ	ـَاتٍ	مَرَرْتُ بِمُسْلِمَاتٍ	رَأَيْتُ مُسْلِمَاتٍ	هُنَّ مُسْلِمَاتٌ
جَمْعُ الْمُذَكَّرِ السَّالِمُ	ـُونَ	ـِينَ	ـِينَ	مَرَرْتُ بِمُسْلِمِينَ	رَأَيْتُ مُسْلِمِينَ	جَاءَ مُسْلِمُونَ
عِشْرُونَ إِلَى تِسْعُونَ – سِنُونَ	ـُونَ	ـِينَ	ـِينَ	مَرَرْتُ بِعِشْرِينَ رَجُلًا	رَأَيْتُ عِشْرِينَ رَجُلًا	جَاءَ عِشْرُونَ رَجُلًا
أُولُو (plural of ذُو)	ـُو	ـِي	ـِي	مَرَرْتُ بِأُولِي مَالٍ	رَأَيْتُ أُولِي مَالٍ	جَاءَ أُولُو مَالٍ
جَمْعُ الْمُذَكَّرِ السَّالِمُ (مُضَافٌ إِلَى يَاءِ الْمُتَكَلِّمِ)	hidden	ـيَّ	ـيَّ	هٰؤُلَاءِ مُسْلِمِيَّ [33]	رَأَيْتُ مُسْلِمِيَّ [34]	مَرَرْتُ بِمُسْلِمِيَّ

EXERCISE[35]

1. Translate, fill in the *i'raab* and identify which rule from among those given in Table 2.11, is applicable.

    i. نجى الفتى من الغرق

    ii. الاقتصاد سبيل الغنى

    iii. نحترم القاضى

    iv. ناديت العاملين

    v. كان التلاميذ منتبهين

    vi. هجم الثعلب على الدجاجات

    vii. اغسل فاك بعد كل طعام

---

[33] مُسْلِمِيَّ was originally مُسْلِمُوْيَ. First, the ن was dropped because of إِضَافَةٌ. It became مُسْلِمُوْيَ. Then, the و was changed to a ي and the two were joined according to the following morphological (صَرْفِيٌّ) rule: "when a و and a ي appear together and the first is سَاكِنٌ, then the و is changed to a ي, and the two ي are joined (this is called إِدْغَامٌ), and the *dammah* before the و is changed into a *kasrah*." Thus, it became مُسْلِمِيَّ.

[34] مُسْلِمِيَّ was originally مُسْلِمِيْنِيَ. First, the ن was dropped because of إِضَافَةٌ. It became مُسْلِمِيْيَ. Then, the two ي were joined (إِدْغَامٌ). Thus, it became مُسْلِمِيَّ.

[35] For more exercises, refer to *al-Nahw al-Wadih, Ibtida'iyyah*, vol. 2, 13-51 & 83-94.

CHAPTER 3
Further Discussion of Nouns

Section 3.1
اَلْاِسْمُ الْمَنْسُوْبُ – Relative Adjective

<u>Definition</u>: It is that noun, which shows something or someone to be related to it.

e.g.	بَغْدَادِيٌّ	someone or something from Baghdad
	صَرْفِيٌّ	an expert in morphology
	نَحْوِيٌّ	an expert in Arabic grammar
	هِنْدِيٌّ	someone or something from India

<u>Rules of Forming</u> اَلْاِسْمُ الْمَنْسُوْبُ:

To show this relation, a يّ (يَاءُ النِّسْبَةِ الْمُشَدَّدَةُ) preceded by a *kasrah* is added at the end of the noun after affecting the following changes, if needed:

1. If a three-letter or a four-letter noun ends with an اَلْأَلِفُ الْمَقْصُوْرَةُ (ى), then (ى) should be changed to a و.

    e.g. عِيْسَى becomes عِيْسَوِيٌّ

    <u>Note</u>: In the case of a five-letter noun, the اَلْأَلِفُ الْمَقْصُوْرَةُ (ى) should be dropped.

    e.g. مُصْطَفَى becomes مُصْطَفِيٌّ

2. If a noun ends with an اَلْأَلِفُ الْمَمْدُوْدَةُ (اء), then the ء should be changed to a و.

    e.g. سَمَاءٌ becomes سَمَاوِيٌّ

3. That noun which already ends with a ي does not require يَاءُ النِّسْبَةِ.

    e.g. شَافِعِيٌّ would remain as is.

4. The round ة at the end of a noun should be dropped.

    e.g. مَكَّةُ becomes مَكِّيٌّ   فَاطِمَةُ becomes فَاطِمِيٌّ

5. The round ة and ي of a noun, which appears on the وَزْن of فَعِيْلَة and فُعَيْلَة should be dropped.

    e.g. مَدِيْنَةُ becomes مَدَنِيٌّ   جُهَيْنَةُ becomes جُهَنِيٌّ

6. In case of the noun, which appears on the وَزْنٌ of فَعِيْلٌ and ends with a ي, the first ي should be changed to a و preceded by a *fathah*, and the second ي should be dropped.

   e.g. (عَلِيْيٌ) عَلِيٌّ becomes عَلَوِيٌّ

7. If the fourth letter of a noun is a ي preceded by a *kasrah*, then the ي can be dropped or it can be changed to a و.

   e.g. دِهْلِيْ becomes دِهْلِيٌّ or دِهْلَوِيٌّ

8. If an original letter from the end of a noun was dropped, it should first be brought back, and then, the relative adjective should be made.

   e.g. أَبٌ (originally أَبَوٌ) becomes أَبَوِيٌّ
   أَخٌ (originally أَخَوٌ) becomes أَخَوِيٌّ
   دَمٌ (originally دَمَوٌ) becomes دَمَوِيٌّ

9. Some words do not follow any particular rule. They are based on usage.

   e.g. نُوْرٌ becomes نُوْرَانِيٌّ   حَقٌّ becomes حَقَّانِيٌّ

EXERCISE

1. Form the relative adjective from the following words.

   i. نَبِي
   ii. مِصر
   iii. بيضاء
   iv. موسى
   v. كوفة

Section 3.2

اَلْاِسْمُ الْتَصْغِيرُ – Diminutive Noun

Definition: It is that noun, which is used to express the diminutive form of a noun. Sometimes, the purpose is to show affection or contempt.

Rules:
1. A three-letter noun would come on the *wazn* of فُعَيْلٌ (or فُعَيْلَةٌ for feminine).

   e.g. رَجُلٌ   becomes   رُجَيْلٌ (a little man)

   عَبْدٌ   becomes   عُبَيْدٌ (a little slave)

2. A four-letter noun would come on the *wazn* of فُعَيْعِلٌ.

   e.g. جَعْفَرٌ   becomes   جُعَيْفِرٌ

3. A five-letter noun, without a و, ا or ي as the fourth, would also come on the *wazn* of فُعَيْعِلٌ. The fifth letter would be dropped.

   e.g. سَفَرْجَلٌ (name of a plant)   becomes   سُفَيْرِجٌ

   A five-letter noun, having a و, ا or ي as the fourth letter, would come on the scale of فُعَيْعِيلٌ.

   e.g. قِرْطَاسٌ (paper)   becomes   قُرَيْطِيسٌ

Notes:
1. In the diminutive form, the hidden ة of a مُؤَنَّثٌ سَمَاعِيٌّ becomes apparent.

   e.g. شَمْسٌ   becomes   شُمَيْسَةٌ

2. In the diminutive form, the last letter of a noun which has been dropped becomes apparent.

   e.g. اِبْنٌ (originally بَنْوٌ)   becomes   بُنَيٌّ

   (بُنَيٌّ was originally بُنَيْوٌ, and underwent a morphological process to become بُنَيٌّ)

EXERCISE

1. Form the diminutive noun from the following words.

   i.   عقرب   iv. كلب
   ii. سلطان   v.   أرض
   iii. عصفور   vi. قمر

Section 3.3
اَلْمَعْرِفَةُ وَالنَّكِرَةُ – Definite and Common Nouns

اَلنَّكِرَةُ (common noun): It is that noun, which denotes something unspecified.

    e.g.   رَجُلٌ   **a man**

اَلْمَعْرِفَةُ (definite noun): It is that noun which denotes something specific. There are seven types of مَعْرِفَةٌ.

1. ضَمِيْرٌ : It is a personal pronoun. It has been discussed earlier in Section 2.4.1.

2. عَلَمٌ : It is a proper noun, i.e. the name of a specific person, place or thing.

    e.g.   زَيْدٌ   مَكَّةُ   زَمْزَمُ

3. اِسْمُ الْإِشَارَةِ : It is the demonstrative pronoun. It has been discussed earlier in section 2.4.3.

4. اَلْاِسْمُ الْمَوْصُوْلُ : It is the relative pronoun. It has been discussed earlier in Section 2.4.2.

5. اَلْمُعَرَّفُ بِاللَّامِ : It is that noun, which has ال (definite particle) at the beginning.

    e.g.   اَلرَّجُلُ   **the man**

6. That common noun (نَكِرَةٌ) which is *mudaaf* to any of the above five definite nouns.

    e.g.   كِتَابُكَ   كِتَابُ زَيْدٍ

            كِتَابُ الَّذِيْ   كِتَابُ هٰذَا الرَّجُلِ

            كِتَابُ الرَّجُلِ

7. اَلْمُنَادَى : It is the vocative noun, i.e. that noun, which appears after a حَرْفُ نِدَاءٍ.

    e.g.   يَا رَجُلُ

EXERCISE

1. Which of the following words are *ma'rifah* (state what type) and which are *nakirah*.

    i. الفرس   v. مكة

    ii. نحن   vi. ذلك

    iii. سيارة الذي   vii. سمك

    iv. يا ولد   viii. سيف الرجل

Section 3.4
اَلْاِسْمُ الْمُذَكَّرُ وَالْمُؤَنَّثُ – Masculine and Feminine Noun

اَلْاِسْمُ الْمُذَكَّرُ - **Masculine Noun:** It is that noun, which does not have any sign from amongst the signs of femininity (عَلَامَاتُ التَّأْنِيْثِ).

اَلْاِسْمُ الْمُؤَنَّثُ - **Feminine Noun:** It is that noun, which has a sign from amongst the signs of femininity. This sign could be apparent or hidden.

عَلَامَاتُ التَّأْنِيْثِ: The signs of being feminine are of two types:

1. لَفْظِيٌّ (in words): It is that sign, which is visible in words. These signs are of the following three types:
   - ة: This renders the word اَلْاِسْمُ الْمُؤَنَّثُ even if the ة appears in a masculine proper noun. e.g. سَيَّارَةٌ   طَلْحَةُ (a masculine proper noun)
   - اَلْأَلِفُ الْمَقْصُوْرَةُ (ى) e.g. صُغْرَى   حُبْلَى
   - اَلْأَلِفُ الْمَمْدُوْدَةُ (اء) e.g. بَيْضَاءُ   حَمْرَاءُ

   If a word has any of these three signs it will be اَلْاِسْمُ الْمُؤَنَّثُ.

2. تَقْدِيْرِيٌّ (assumed): It is that sign, which is not visible in words and is assumed to exist. This is determined by looking at the diminutive form (تَصْغِيْرٌ) of a particular word. This reveals the original letters of the word.
   - e.g. أَرْضٌ   The diminutive form is أُرَيْضَةٌ. Therefore, it is اَلْاِسْمُ الْمُؤَنَّثُ.
   - شَمْسٌ   The diminutive form is شُمَيْسَةٌ. Therefore, it is اَلْاِسْمُ الْمُؤَنَّثُ.

Based on the signs of femininity being لَفْظِيٌّ or تَقْدِيْرِيٌّ, اَلْاِسْمُ الْمُؤَنَّثُ is of two types:

1. اَلْمُؤَنَّثُ الْقِيَاسِيُّ (according to rule): It is that feminine noun, which has a لَفْظِيٌّ sign of femininity.
2. اَلْمُؤَنَّثُ السَّمَاعِيُّ (according to usage): It is that feminine noun, which has a تَقْدِيْرِيٌّ sign of femininity.

In terms of ذَاتٌ (essence), اَلْاِسْمُ الْمُؤَنَّثُ is of two types:

1. مُؤَنَّثٌ حَقِيْقِيٌّ: It is that feminine noun, which has an opposite masculine.
   - e.g. اِمْرَأَةٌ (woman). Its masculine is رَجُلٌ (man).
2. مُؤَنَّثٌ لَفْظِيٌّ: It is that feminine noun, which does not have an opposite masculine.
   - e.g. ظُلْمَةٌ (darkness)   عَيْنٌ (spring)

Notes:
1. The following are used as feminine (مُؤَنَّثٌ):
   a. Name of females.
      e.g. زَيْنَبُ   مَرْيَمُ
   b. Words denoting the feminine gender.
      e.g. أُخْتٌ   أُمٌّ
   c. Names of countries, cities, towns and tribes.
      e.g. قُرَيْشٌ   مِصْرُ
   d. Parts of the body found in pairs.
      e.g. يَدٌ   أُذُنٌ

      Note: There are exceptions to the rule. خَدٌّ (cheek), حَاجِبٌ (eyebrow) etc. are masculine.
   e. Names of various types of winds.
      e.g. صَرْصَرٌ   رِيحٌ
   f. Various names of *Jahannam* (hell).
      e.g. سَقَرُ   جَهَنَّمُ
   g. Letters of the alphabet (اَلْحُرُوفُ الْهِجَائِيَّةُ) are generally used as مُؤَنَّثٌ. They can also be used as masculine.
      e.g. ا   ب   ت   ....

2. There are some words that Arabs use as feminine without regard to the presence or absence of signs of femininity. Examples include the following:

   دَلْوٌ (bucket)   حَرْثٌ (tillage/field)   بِئْرٌ (well)
   نَفْسٌ (self)   نَارٌ (fire)   دَارٌ (house)

Section 3.5

وَاحِدٌ وَتَثْنِيَةٌ وَجَمْعٌ – Singular, Dual and Plural

وَاحِدٌ – Singular: It is that noun, which denotes one.

e.g.   رَجُلٌ   one man

تَثْنِيَةٌ – Dual: It is that noun, which denotes two. It is formed by placing at the end of a singular (وَاحِدٌ) one of the following:

- An أَلِفٌ preceded by a *fathah* and followed by a نُوْنٌ with a *kasrah* i.e. [ـَانِ] for حَالَةُ الرَّفْعِ. (أَلِفٌ مَا قَبْلَهَا مَفْتُوْحٌ وَبَعْدَهَا نُوْنٌ مَكْسُوْرَةٌ)

    e.g.   رَجُلَانِ   two men

- A يَاءٌ preceded by a *fathah* and followed by نُوْنٌ with a *kasrah* i.e. [ـَيْنِ] for حَالَةُ النَّصْبِ (يَاءٌ مَا قَبْلَهَا مَفْتُوْحٌ وَبَعْدَهَا نُوْنٌ مَكْسُوْرَةٌ). وَالْجَرِّ

    e.g.   رَجُلَيْنِ   two men

جَمْعٌ – Plural: It is that noun, which denotes more than two.

e.g.   رِجَالٌ   men

Note: The نُوْنٌ of تَثْنِيَةٌ and جَمْعٌ is dropped in case of إِضَافَةٌ.

e.g.   قَلَمَا زَيْدٍ   (Originally, قَلَمَانِ زَيْدٍ but the نُوْنٌ was dropped due to إِضَافَةٌ.)

فَرَسَا رَجُلٍ   (Originally, فَرَسَانِ رَجُلٍ but the نُوْنٌ was dropped due to إِضَافَةٌ.)

مُسْلِمُوْ مِصْرَ   (Originally, مُسْلِمُوْنَ مِصْرَ but the نُوْنٌ was dropped due to إِضَافَةٌ.)

طَالِبُوْ عِلْمٍ (Originally, طَالِبُوْنَ عِلْمٍ but the نُوْنٌ was dropped due to إِضَافَةٌ.)

EXERCISE

1. Translate the following into Arabic.
    i. The boy's two bicycles.
    ii. The farmer's two servants.
    iii. Your parents came.
    iv. I saw your parents.
    v. The servants of *deen*.
    vi. The teachers of the school.

Section 3.6
أَقْسَامُ الجَمْعِ – Types of Plural

<u>اَلجَمْعُ السَّالِمُ</u> – **Sound Plural:** It is that plural whose صِيغَةٌ (letter sequence/form) of وَاحِدٌ does not change, when its plural is made. In other words, the singular letter sequence does not break.

e.g. مُسْلِمُوْنَ   (singular – مُسْلِمٌ)

There are two types of اَلجَمْعُ السَّالِمُ:

1. جَمْعُ مُذَكَّرٍ سَالِمٌ – **Masculine Sound Plural:** It is formed by adding at the end of a singular (وَاحِدٌ) one of the following:

    - A وَاوٌ preceded by a *dammah* and followed by a نُوْنٌ with a *fathah* i.e. [ـُوْنَ] for (وَاوٌ مَا قَبْلَهَا مَضْمُوْمٌ وَبَعْدَهَا نُوْنٌ مَفْتُوْحَةٌ). حَالَةُ الرَّفْعِ
    e.g. مُسْلِمُوْنَ

    - A يَاءٌ preceded by a *kasrah* and followed by a نُوْنٌ with a *fathah* i.e. [ـِيْنَ] for (يَاءٌ مَا قَبْلَهَا مَكْسُوْرٌ وَبَعْدَهَا نُوْنٌ مَفْتُوْحَةٌ). حَالَةُ النَّصْبِ وَالجَرِّ
    e.g. مُسْلِمِيْنَ

2. جَمْعُ مُؤَنَّثٍ سَالِمٌ – **Feminine Sound Plural:** It is formed by discarding the round ة and adding at the end of a singular, one of the following:

    - An أَلِفٌ preceded by a *fathah* and followed by a *madmoom* long ت i.e. [ـَاتٌ] for (أَلِفٌ مَا قَبْلَهَا مَفْتُوْحٌ وَبَعْدَهَا تَاءٌ مَضْمُوْمَةٌ). حَالَةُ الرَّفْعِ
    e.g. مُسْلِمَاتٌ

    - An أَلِفٌ preceded by a *fathah* and followed by a *maksoor* long ت i.e. [ـَاتٍ] for (أَلِفٌ مَا قَبْلَهَا مَفْتُوْحٌ وَبَعْدَهَا تَاءٌ مَكْسُوْرَةٌ). حَالَةُ النَّصْبِ وَ الجَرِّ
    e.g. مُسْلِمَاتٍ

<u>اَلجَمْعُ المُكَسَّرُ</u> – **Broken Plural:** It is that plural whose صِيغَةٌ (the singular letter sequence/form) of وَاحِدٌ changes, when its plural is made. In other words, the singular letter sequence breaks.

e.g. رِجَالٌ   (singular – رَجُلٌ)

جَمْعُ قِلَّةٍ – **Restricted Plural:** It is that plural, which denotes a number from three to ten. It has four common أَوْزَانٌ.

Table 3.1
أَوْزَانُ جَمْعِ قِلَّةٍ

Wazn	Examples		
	Singular	Meaning	Plural
أَفْعُلٌ	نَفْسٌ	self	أَنْفُسٌ
أَفْعَالٌ	قَوْلٌ	statement	أَقْوَالٌ
أَفْعِلَةٌ	طَعَامٌ	food	أَطْعِمَةٌ
فِعْلَةٌ	غُلَامٌ	boy	غِلْمَةٌ

Note: The masculine and feminine sound plural, which is **not** preceded by an ال is also considered جَمْعُ قِلَّةٍ.

e.g. عَاقِلَاتٌ intelligent females   عَاقِلُونَ intelligent males

جَمْعُ كَثْرَةٍ – **Unrestricted Plural:** It is that plural, which denotes a number from three upwards. Some of the common أَوْزَانٌ are given below.

Table 3.2
أَوْزَانُ جَمْعِ كَثْرَةٍ

Wazn	Examples		
	Singular	Meaning	Plural
فِعَالٌ	عَبْدٌ	slave	عِبَادٌ
فُعَلَاءُ	عَلِيمٌ	knowledgeable	عُلَمَاءُ
أَفْعِلَاءُ	نَبِيٌّ	prophet	أَنْبِيَاءُ
فُعُلٌ	رَسُولٌ	messenger	رُسُلٌ
فُعُولٌ	نَجْمٌ	star	نُجُومٌ
فُعَّالٌ	خَادِمٌ	servant	خُدَّامٌ
فَعْلَى	مَرِيضٌ	patient	مَرْضَى
فَعَلَةٌ	طَالِبٌ	student	طَلَبَةٌ
فِعَلٌ	فِرْقَةٌ	group/sect	فِرَقٌ
فِعْلَانٌ	غُلَامٌ	boy	غِلْمَانٌ

Note: The masculine and feminine sound plural which is preceded by an ال is also considered as جَمْعُ كَثْرَةٍ.

e.g. اَلْمُسْلِمَاتُ   اَلْمُسْلِمُونَ

جَمْعُ الْجَمْعِ – **Plural of a Plural:** It is the plural of a plural. Sometimes, it appears on the *wazn* of مُنْتَهَى الْجُمُوعِ and sometimes on the *wazn* of اَلْجَمْعُ السَّالِمُ. Not every plural has a plural. Some examples of plurals, which have a plural are given below.

Table 3.3
أَمْثَالُ جَمْعِ الْجَمْعِ

Singular	Meaning	Plural	Plural of Plural
نِعْمَةٌ	blessing	أَنْعُمٌ	أَنَاعِيمُ
ظُفْرٌ	nail	أَظْفَارُ	أَظَافِيرُ
بَيْتٌ	house	بُيُوتٌ	بُيُوتَاتٌ
فَاضِلٌ	well-qualified	أَفَاضِلُ	أَفَاضِلُونَ

مُنْتَهَى الْجُمُوعِ: It is that plural, which has after the أَلِفُ الْجَمْعِ (*alif* of plural), one of the following:

- two مُتَحَرِّكُ letters.   e.g. مَسَاجِدُ
- one مُشَدَّدٌ letter.   e.g. دَوَابُّ (the original being دَوَابِبُ)
- three letters, the middle one being سَاكِنٌ.   e.g. مَفَاتِيحُ

Some of the common *wazns* of مُنْتَهَى الْجُمُوعِ are given below:

Table 3.4
أَوْزَانُ مُنْتَهَى الْجُمُوعِ

Wazn	Examples		
	Singular	Meaning	Plural
مَفَاعِلُ	مَسْجِدٌ	mosque	مَسَاجِدُ
مَفَاعِيلُ	مِفْتَاحٌ	key	مَفَاتِيحُ
فَوَاعِلُ	قَاعِدَةٌ	rule/maxim	قَوَاعِدُ
فَعَائِلُ	رِسَالَةٌ	message/letter	رَسَائِلُ
أَفَاعِلُ	أَكْبَرُ	elder	أَكَابِرُ

اِسْمُ الْجَمْعِ – **Collective Noun:**[36] It is a singular noun, which gives a plural meaning. Generally, it does not have a singular from the same word.

    e.g.   قَوْمٌ   nation

              رَهْطٌ   group

Note:
1. These words have plurals.

    e.g.   قَوْمٌ ⟶ أَقْوَامٌ   رَهْطٌ ⟶ أَرْهَاطٌ

2. In usage, if the **word** is considered, it will be used as a singular noun.

    e.g.   اَلْقَوْمُ حَاضِرٌ   The people are present.

    If its **meaning** is considered (as is commonly done), it will be used as a plural noun.

    e.g.   قَوْمٌ صَالِحُوْنَ   righteous people

Notes:
1. Some plurals do not have the same root letters as their singulars.

    e.g.   اِمْرَأَةٌ   (woman) ⟶ نِسَاءٌ

          ذُوْ   (the one who possesses something) ⟶ أُولُوْ

2. Some plurals are not according to rule (خِلَافُ الْقِيَاسِ).

    e.g.   أُمٌّ   (mother) ⟶ أُمَّهَاتٌ

          فَمٌّ   (mouth) ⟶ أَفْوَاهٌ

          مَاءٌ   (water) ⟶ مِيَاهٌ

          إِنْسَانٌ   (human being) ⟶ أُنَاسٌ

          شَاةٌ   (goat/sheep) ⟶ شِيَاهٌ

اِسْمُ الْجِنْسِ – **Generic Noun:**[37] It is that noun, which is devised for an essence (مَاهِيَّة). Because of that, it refers to an entire genus (category/class). Generally, its singular has a (ة). For example,

شَجَرٌ refers to trees. Its singular is شَجَرَةٌ (a tree).

نَخْلٌ refers to date-palm trees. Its singular is نَخْلَةٌ (a date-palm tree).

---

[36] For more details, please refer to 'Abd al-Ghaniyy al-Daqr, *Mu'jam al-Qawa'id al-'Arabiyyah fi al-Nahw wa al-Tasreef*, (Damascus: Dar al-Qalam, 1986), 36.

[37] For more details, please refer to *Mu'jam al-Qawa'id al-'Arabiyyah*, 36.

EXERCISE

1. What type of plurals are the following?

    i. صائمات   ii. جيش   iii. أكلب

    iv. مصابيح   v. بلاد   vi. كتب

    vii. صائمون   viii. إبل   ix. غنم

Section 3.7
اَلْمَرْفُوعَاتُ - Words That Are Always *Marfoo'*

There are eight words that are always in the state of رَفْعٌ. These are as follows:

1. فَاعِلٌ 2. نَائِبُ الْفَاعِلِ 3. مُبْتَدَأٌ 4. خَبَرٌ 5. خَبَرُ إِنَّ وَأَخَوَاتِهَا
6. اِسْمُ كَانَ وَأَخَوَاتِهَا 7. اِسْمُ مَا وَلَا الْمُشَبَّهَتَيْنِ بِلَيْسَ 8. خَبَرُ لَا الَّتِي لِنَفْيِ الْجِنْسِ

Some of these have been discussed before. مُبْتَدَأٌ (subject) and خَبَرٌ (predicate) were discussed in Section 1.4.1, خَبَرُ إِنَّ وَأَخَوَاتِهَا was discussed in Section 1.8, and اِسْمُ كَانَ وَأَخَوَاتِهَا was discussed in Section 1.9. We discuss the rest below.

Section 3.7.1
فَاعِلٌ — Subject/Doer

Definition: It is the doer of the action or of the meaning contained in the verb.

- The فَاعِلٌ can either be a personal pronoun or an اِسْمٌ ظَاهِرٌ (i.e. visible in words after the فِعْلٌ). We have discussed personal pronouns before in Section 2.4.1. Now, we will discuss what the فِعْلٌ should be for various types of فَاعِلٌ.

Table 3.5
اِسْتِعْمَالُ الْفِعْلِ حَسْبَ الْفَاعِلِ

	If the فَاعِلٌ is	Then the فِعْلٌ will be	Example
1.	ظَاهِرٌ مُؤَنَّثٌ حَقِيقِيٌّ and there is no word between the فِعْلٌ and the فَاعِلٌ.	وَاحِدٌ مُؤَنَّثٌ	قَامَتْ عَائِشَةُ
2.	ضَمِيرٌ مُؤَنَّثٌ	مُؤَنَّثٌ and its singularity, duality, or plurality will be according to the preceding noun that it refers to.	اَلْمُعَلِّمَةُ نَصَرَتْ - اَلْمُعَلِّمَتَانِ نَصَرَتَا - اَلْمُعَلِّمَاتُ نَصَرْنَ
3.	ظَاهِرٌ مُؤَنَّثٌ حَقِيقِيٌّ and there is a word between the فِعْلٌ and the فَاعِلٌ.	وَاحِدٌ مُؤَنَّثٌ or وَاحِدٌ مُذَكَّرٌ	قَرَأَ الْيَوْمَ عَائِشَةُ or قَرَأَتِ الْيَوْمَ عَائِشَةُ
4.	ظَاهِرٌ مُؤَنَّثٌ غَيْرُ حَقِيقِيٍّ	وَاحِدٌ مُؤَنَّثٌ or وَاحِدٌ مُذَكَّرٌ	طَلَعَتِ الشَّمْسُ or طَلَعَ الشَّمْسُ
5.	ظَاهِرٌ جَمْعُ مُكَسَّرٍ	وَاحِدٌ مُؤَنَّثٌ or وَاحِدٌ مُذَكَّرٌ	قَالَتِ الرِّجَالُ or قَالَ الرِّجَالُ

Table 3.5 – *Continued*

If the فَاعِلٌ is	Then the فِعْلٌ will be	Example
6. any اِسْمٌ ظَاهِرٌ beside the above five categories	وَاحِدٌ corresponding in gender	ضَرَبَ الرَّجُلُ – ضَرَبَ الرَّجُلَانِ – ضَرَبَ الرِّجَالُ
7. ضَمِيْرٌ مُذَكَّرٌ	مُذَكَّرٌ and its singularity, duality, or plurality will be according to the preceding noun that it refers to	اَلْخَادِمُ ذَهَبَ – اَلْخَادِمَانِ ذَهَبَا – اَلْخَادِمُوْنَ ذَهَبُوْا
8. ضَمِيْرٌ جَمْعٌ مُكَسَّرٌ	وَاحِدٌ مُؤَنَّثٌ or جَمْعٌ مُذَكَّرٌ	اَلرِّجَالُ قَامَتْ or اَلرِّجَالُ قَامُوْا

EXERCISE

1. Fill in a suitable فِعْلٌ in the spaces below.

   i. الولدان _____ ii. _____/_____ الطلابُ

   iii. _____ النساء iv. _____/_____ السفينة

   v. الأطفال _____/_____ vi. _____/_____ اليوم امرأةٌ

Section 3.7.2
Substitute of فَاعِلٌ – مَفْعُوْلُ مَا لَمْ يُسَمَّ فَاعِلُهُ / نَائِبُ الْفَاعِلِ

Definition: It is that noun, which is the فَاعِلٌ of a فِعْلٌ مَجْهُوْلٌ (passive voice). The original فَاعِلٌ is dropped and the مَفْعُوْلٌ بِهِ subsitutes it. This is why, it is called نَائِبُ الْفَاعِلِ (substitute of فَاعِلٌ) or مَفْعُوْلٌ (the مَفْعُوْلٌ of such a فِعْلٌ whose فَاعِلٌ is not mentioned).

e.g.   ضُرِبَ زَيْدٌ   Zayd was hit. (The doer is not known/mentioned.)

The same فِعْلٌ – فَاعِلٌ usage rules apply as mentioned above in Table 3.5.

e.g.
1. نُصِرَتْ عَائِشَةُ
2. عَائِشَةُ نُصِرَتْ
3. نُصِرَ الْيَوْمَ عَائِشَةُ or نُصِرَتِ الْيَوْمَ عَائِشَةُ
4. رُئِيَ الشَّمْسُ or رُئِيَتِ الشَّمْسُ
5. ضُرِبَ الرِّجَالُ or ضُرِبَتِ الرِّجَالُ
6. ضُرِبَ الرَّجُلُ or ضُرِبَ الرَّجُلَانِ or ضُرِبَ الرِّجَالُ
7. اَلْخَادِمُ طُلِبَ or اَلْخَادِمَانِ طُلِبَا or اَلْخَادِمُوْنَ طُلِبُوْا
8. اَلرِّجَالُ ضُرِبَتْ or اَلرِّجَالُ ضُرِبُوْا

Sentence Analysis:

الْبَابُ	فُتِحَ	The door was opened.
نَائِبُ الْفَاعِلِ	فِعْلٌ مَجْهُوْلٌ	

EXERCISE

1. Convert the following to فِعْلٌ مَجْهُوْلٌ with its نَائِبُ الْفَاعِلِ.

    i. سرق اللص المال   iii. نعبد الله

    ii. فتح زيد الأبواب   iv. ذبح الرجل الشاة

2. Convert the following to فِعْلٌ – فَاعِلٌ – مَفْعُوْلٌ.

    i. تُحْلَبُ البقرة   iii. سُئِلَ المعلم

    ii. قُطِعَتِ الزهرة   iv. شُرِبَ اللبن

Section 3.7.3[38]
اِسْمُ مَا وَلَا الْمُشَبَّهَتَيْنِ بِلَيْسَ – The Noun of Those مَا and لَا, Which Are Similar to لَيْسَ

- It means that مَا and لَا have the same meaning and effect (عَمَلٌ) as لَيْسَ.

  e.g. مَا زَيْدٌ قَائِمًا   Zayd is not standing.

  لَا رَجُلٌ أَفْضَلَ مِنْكَ   No man is more virtuous than you.

- Like لَيْسَ, sometimes, an extra *baa'* (بَاءٌ زَائِدَةٌ) is added before the خَبَر.

  e.g. مَا أَنَا بِقَارِئٍ   I am not a reader/I cannot read.

- The effect of مَا and لَا will be cancelled if any of the following occurs:

  i. When the خَبَر appears before the اِسْم.

       e.g. مَا قَائِمٌ زَيْدٌ   Zayd is not standing.

  ii. The word إِلَّا appears before the خَبَر negating the negative meaning of مَا and لَا.

       e.g. مَا مُحَمَّدٌ إِلَّا رَسُولٌ   And Muhammad is not but a messenger./
  And Muhammad is only a messenger.
  [Allah bless him and give him peace]

  iii. If the اِسْم and/or خَبَر of لَا is not نَكِرَة. (مَا can appear before a مَعْرِفَة or a نَكِرَة)

       e.g. لَا الْمَدِينَةُ كَبِيرَةٌ   The city is not big.

---

[38] For more details, examples and exercises, please refer to *al-Nahw al-Wadih, Thanawiyyah*, vol. 1, 95-102.

Section 3.7.4[39]

خَبَرُ لَا الَّتِيْ لِنَفْيِ الْجِنْسِ – The خَبَر of That لَا Which Negates an Entire جِنْسٌ (Category/Class)

- لَا gives its اِسْم a single *fathah* and its خَبَر a *dammah* when the اِسْم and the خَبَر are نَكِرَةٌ.

    e.g. لَا رَجُلَ قَائِمٌ   No man is standing.

Table 3.6
Different Forms of the Noun of لَا and Its *I'raab*

	If the اِسْم of لَا is	Then it will be	Explanation	Example
1.	شِبْهُ الْمُضَافِ [40] or مُضَافٌ	مَنْصُوبٌ		لَا خَادِمَ رَجُلٍ فِي الدَّارِ There is no servant of a man in the house. لَا سَاعِيًا خَيْرًا مَذْمُومٌ No one who attempts to do good is blameworthy.
2.	نَكِرَةٌ مُفْرَدَةٌ	مَبْنِيٌّ عَلَى الْفَتْحِ		لَا رَجُلَ فِي الدَّارِ There is no man in the house.
3.	مَعْرِفَةٌ	مَرْفُوعٌ	- The لَا has to be repeated with another مَعْرِفَةٌ. - The effect of لَا is cancelled.	لَا زَيْدٌ فِي الدَّارِ وَلَا عَمْرٌو Neither is Zayd in the house nor 'Amr.
4.	نَكِرَةٌ with a word between it and لَا	مَرْفُوعٌ	- The لَا has to be repeated. - The effect of لَا is cancelled.	لَا فِيهَا رَجُلٌ وَلَا امْرَأَةٌ Neither is there a man in it nor a woman.
5.	لَا and نَكِرَةٌ repeated with no word between them	فَتْحُهُمَا رَفْعُهُمَا فَتْحُ الْأَوَّلِ وَنَصْبُ الثَّانِي فَتْحُ الْأَوَّلِ وَرَفْعُ الثَّانِي رَفْعُ الْأَوَّلِ وَفَتْحُ الثَّانِي		لَا حَوْلَ وَلَا قُوَّةَ [41] لَا حَوْلٌ وَلَا قُوَّةٌ لَا حَوْلَ وَلَا قُوَّةٌ لَا حَوْلَ وَلَا قُوَّةٌ لَا حَوْلٌ وَلَا قُوَّةَ

---

[39] For more details, examples and exercises, please refer to *al-Nahw al-Wadih*, *Thanawiyyah*, vol. 1, 118-122.

[40] It refers to the case when a word is connected to another word, which completes its meaning, in the same way that *mudaaf* and *mudaaf ilayhi* are connected to one another.

[41] There is no power (to do good) and there is no power (to stay away from evil) [except with Allah's help].

Note: The خَبَر of لا may be omitted when the meaning is understood.

e.g. لا بَأْسَ   i.e. لا بَأْسَ عَلَيْكَ   There is no harm upon you. / No problem.

EXERCISE

1. Translate, fill in the *i'raab* and point out the rule which applies.

   i. لا خير فى مال البخيل لنفسه
   ii. لا طالب علم فى الفصل
   iii. لا صاحب جُود مذموم
   iv. لا الرجل كريم ولا ابنه
   v. لا بكر فى الفصل ولا حسن
   vi. لا فى الفصل معلم ولا طالب
   vii. لا دار كتب في المدينة
   viii. لا في الحديقة صبيان ولا بنات

Section 3.8

اَلْمَنْصُوْبَاتُ – Words Which Are Always *Mansoob*[42]

1. مَفْعُوْلٌ بِهِ
2. مَفْعُوْلٌ مُطْلَقٌ
3. مَفْعُوْلٌ لَهُ   } known as اَلْمَفَاعِيْلُ الْخَمْسَةُ
4. مَفْعُوْلٌ مَعَهُ
5. مَفْعُوْلٌ فِيْهِ
6. اَلْحَالُ

7. اَلتَّمْيِيْزُ / اَلتَّمْيِيْزُ
8. اِسْمُ إِنَّ وَأَخَوَاتِهَا
9. خَبَرُ مَا وَلَا الْمُشَبَّهَتَيْنِ بِلَيْسَ
10. اِسْمُ لَا الَّتِي لِنَفْيِ الْجِنْسِ
11. خَبَرُ كَانَ وَأَخَوَاتِهَا
12. اَلْمُسْتَثْنَى

Of these, 8, 9, 10 and 11 have been discussed before. Here, we will discuss the remaining.

Section 3.8.1
مَفْعُوْلٌ بِهِ – Object

Definition: It is that word on which the action of the فَاعِلٌ takes place.

e.g.   شَرِبَ   خَالِدٌ   مَاءً   Khalid drank water.
        فِعْلٌ   فَاعِلٌ   مَفْعُوْلٌ بِهِ

- Sometimes, the verb governing the مَفْعُوْلٌ بِهِ is dropped as in the following:

  a. مُنَادَى (the one being called):[43]

  e.g.   يَا   ابْنَ زَيْدٍ   O son of Zayd!
          حَرْفُ النِّدَاءِ   مُنَادَى (مَفْعُوْلٌ بِهِ)

  It was originally (أَدْعُو ابْنَ زَيْدٍ). The verb أَدْعُو was dropped.

  Note:
  - The حَرْفُ النِّدَاءِ (vocative particle) substitutes the omitted verb.
    Some of the vocative particles are as follows:

    أَيْ and أ   These are used when the مُنَادَى is near.
    هَيَا and أَيَا   These are used when the مُنَادَى is far.
    يَا   This is used for both (near and far).

---

[42] There are exceptions to the rule. *Mustathnaa*, for example, is not always *mansoob*. It is still mentioned under this category because most of the time, it is *mansoob*.

[43] For more details, examples and exercises, please refer to *al-Nahw al-Wadih, Ibtida'iyyah*, vol. 3, 120-124.

Table 3.7
Rules Governing the *I'raab* of the مُنَادَى

If the مُنَادَى is	Then it will be	Example	
1. مُضَافٌ	مَنْصُوبٌ	يَا ابْنَ زَيْدٍ	O son of Zayd!
2. شَبِيهٌ بِالْمُضَافِ [44]	مَنْصُوبٌ	يَا قَارِئًا كِتَابًا	O reader of a book!
3. نَكِرَةٌ غَيْرُ مُعَيَّنَةٍ (Unspecified *nakirah*)	مَنْصُوبٌ	يَا رَجُلًا خُذْ بِيَدِي	O man! Take my hand. (call of a blind man to **any** person for assisstance)
4. نَكِرَةٌ مُعَيَّنَةٌ (Specified *nakirah*)	مَرْفُوعٌ	يَا رَجُلُ	O man!
5. مَعْرِفَةٌ مُفْرَدَةٌ (Singular *ma'rifah*)	مَرْفُوعٌ	يَا زَيْدُ	O Zayd!
6. مُعَرَّفٌ بِـ ال	مَرْفُوعٌ	أَيُّهَا (masculine) or أَيَّتُهَا (feminine) has to be added between the حَرْفُ النِّدَاءِ and مُنَادَى. يَا أَيُّهَا الرَّجُلُ O man! يَا أَيَّتُهَا الْمَرْأَةُ O woman!	

- تَرْخِيمٌ (abbreviation) is allowed in *munaadaa*.

  e.g. يَا مَالِكُ can become يَا مَالِ or يَا مَالُ

  يَا مَنْصُورُ can become يَا مَنْصُ

  Note: The last letter can be given a *dammah* or it can retain its original *harakah*.

b. <u>أَهْلًا وَ سَهْلًا</u>: This is said to one's guest for welcoming him/her.

   Its original is أَتَيْتَ أَهْلًا وَوَطِئْتَ سَهْلًا, which means "You have come to your own people and have trampled comfortable ground." In other words, "you are welcome." Here two verbs, أَتَيْتَ and وَطِئْتَ have been dropped.

c. Sometimes, when warning someone, the verb governing the مَفْعُولٌ بِهِ is dropped due to context. Examples include the following:

   - الطَّرِيقَ الطَّرِيقَ is used instead of اِتَّقِ الطَّرِيقَ to give the same meaning, which is "Beware of the road!" Here, the verb اِتَّقِ has been dropped.
   - إِيَّاكَ وَالْأَسَدَ is used instead of اِتَّقِ نَفْسَكَ مِنَ الْأَسَدِ to give the same meaning, which is "Save yourself from the lion."

---

[44] This is another term for شِبْهُ الْمُضَافِ. As mentioned earlier, it is similar to *mudaaf* in meaning.

Section 3.8.2[45]
مَفْعُولٌ مُطْلَقٌ

Definition: It is the *masdar* of the verb that governs it and is used for the following:

- تَأْكِيدٌ (emphasis)   e.g.   ضَرَبْتُهُ ضَرْبًا   I beat him severely.
- بَيَانُ النَّوْعِ (description of type)   e.g.   جَلَسْتُ جِلْسَةَ الْقَارِئِ   I sat like a *Qari* would sit.
- بَيَانُ الْعَدَدِ (number of times)   e.g.   ضَرَبْتُهُ ضَرْبَتَيْنِ   I hit him twice.

Note: Sometimes, the verb governing مَفْعُولٌ مُطْلَقٌ is dropped because of context. For example, خَيْرَ مَقْدَمٍ. Originally, it was قَدِمْتَ قُدُومًا خَيْرَ مَقْدَمٍ, which means "You came a good coming." Here, the verb قَدِمْتَ, and قُدُومًا, which is the مَفْعُولٌ مُطْلَقٌ, have been dropped because of context. Only the صِفَةٌ of the مَفْعُولٌ مُطْلَقٌ, which is خَيْرَ مَقْدَمٍ, remains.

Section 3.8.3[46]
مَفْعُولٌ لِأَجْلِهِ / مَفْعُولٌ لَهُ

Definition: It is that noun, which explains the reason for the action taking place. Generally, it is a *masdar*.

e.g.   ضَرَبْتُهُ تَأْدِيبًا   I beat/hit him to teach (him) manners.

Section 3.8.4[47]
مَفْعُولٌ مَعَهُ

Definition: It is that noun, which appears after such a وَاوٌ, which has the meaning of مَعَ (with). This وَاوٌ is known as وَاوُ الْمَعِيَّةِ.

e.g.   جَاءَ زَيْدٌ وَالْكِتَابَ   Zayd came <u>with</u> the book.

         جِئْتُ وَزَيْدًا   I came <u>with</u> Zayd.

---

[45] For more details, examples, and exercises, please refer to *al-Nahw al-Wadih*, Ibtida'iyyah, vol. 2, 156-160. For additional types of مَفْعُولٌ مُطْلَقٌ, with accompanying examples and exercises, please refer to *al-Nahw al-Wadih*, Thanawiyyah, vol. 1, 127-130.

[46] For more details, examples, and exercises, please refer to *al-Nahw al-Wadih*, Ibtida'iyyah, vol. 2, 161-164.

[47] For more details, examples and exercises, please refer to *al-Nahw al-Wadih*, Ibtida'iyyah, vol. 3, 157-162.

Section 3.8.5
<u>ظَرْفٌ / مَفْعُولٌ فِيهِ</u>

Definition: It is that noun, which denotes the time (زَمَانٌ) or place (مَكَانٌ) in which an action took place.

  e.g. سَافَرْتُ شَهْرًا I travelled for a month.

  Both types of ظُرُوفٌ, namely, زَمَانٌ and مَكَانٌ are of two types: مَحْدُودٌ (limited, restricted) and مُبْهَمٌ (unlimited, unrestricted).

- <u>Types of ظُرُوفُ الزَّمَانِ</u>

 i. مَحْدُودٌ (limited, restricted): for example,

يَوْمٌ	day	e.g.	صُمْتُ يَوْمًا	I fasted for one day.
لَيْلٌ	night	e.g.	عَمِلْتُ لَيْلًا	I worked for one night.
شَهْرٌ	month	e.g.	صُمْتُ شَهْرًا	I fasted for a month.
سَنَةٌ	year	e.g.	سَافَرْتُ سَنَةً	I travelled for a year.

 ii. مُبْهَمٌ (unlimited, unrestricted): for example,

دَهْرٌ	long period of time

    e.g. صُمْتُ دَهْرًا I fasted for a long time.

حِينٌ	some time (could be short or long period of time)

    e.g. دَعَا نُوحٌ قَوْمَهُ حِينًا مِنَ الدَّهْرِ
    Nuh (peace be upon him) called his people for some time.

- <u>Types of ظُرُوفُ الْمَكَانِ</u>

 i. مَحْدُودٌ (limited, restricted):

  e.g. صَلَّيْتُ فِي الْمَسْجِدِ I prayed in the mosque.
  e.g. جَلَسْتُ فِي الدَّارِ I sat in the house.

 ii. مُبْهَمٌ (unlimited, unrestricted):

خَلْفَ	behind	e.g.	جَلَسْتُ خَلْفَهُ	I sat behind him.
أَمَامَ	in front of	e.g.	قُمْتُ أَمَامَهُ	I stood in front of him.

Note: In the case of مَكَانٌ (مَحْدُودٌ), the preposition فِي is mentioned in words; while in the case of مَكَانٌ (مُبْهَمٌ), it is assumed to exist (مُقَدَّرٌ).

The above-mentioned five *maf'ools* have been combined in a couplet, which is as follows:

$$\text{حَمِدْتُ حَمْدًا حَامِدًا وَحَمِيْدًا}$$
$$\text{رِعَايَةَ شُكْرِهِ دَهْرًا مَدِيْدًا}$$

I praised Haamid a lot, with Hameed,
out of regard for thanking him, for an extended period of time.

Sentence Analysis:

1. مُضَافٌ + مُضَافٌ إِلَيْهِ = شُكْرِهِ

   مُضَافٌ + مُضَافٌ إِلَيْهِ = رِعَايَةَ شُكْرِهِ

2. صِفَةٌ = مَدِيْدًا

   مَوْصُوْفٌ = دَهْرًا

حَمِدْتُ	حَمْدًا	حَامِدًا	وَحَمِيْدًا	رِعَايَةَ شُكْرِهِ	دَهْرًا مَدِيْدًا
(فِعْلٌ + فَاعِلٌ)	مَفْعُوْلٌ مُطْلَقٌ	مَفْعُوْلٌ بِهِ	مَفْعُوْلٌ مَعَهُ	مَفْعُوْلٌ لَهُ	مَفْعُوْلٌ فِيْهِ

= جُمْلَةٌ فِعْلِيَّةٌ خَبَرِيَّةٌ

EXERCISE

1. Translate, fill in the *i'raab* and identify the type of مَفْعُوْلٌ in the following sentences.

   i. أكلَ عليٌّ أكلتين
   ii. ركب إبراهيم الحصان
   iii. سافرت وأخاك
   iv. يثب النمر وثوب الأسد
   v. يسافر خالد إلى مصر طلبا للعلم
   vi. لا تبخلوا خشية الفقر
   vii. توقد المصابيح ليلا
   viii. سافر زيد طالبا للعلم
   ix. وقف الشرطي وقوف النشاط
   x. قرأت الدرس صباحا أمام المعلم
   xi. تدور الأرض دورة في اليوم
   xii. اعملوا الخير حبا في الخير
   xiii. جلست الهرة تحت المكتب
   xiv. سارت السيارة ساعة

Section 3.8.6[48]
حَالٌ – State / Condition

Definition: It is a noun, which describes the condition of either the فَاعِلٌ or the مَفْعُوْلٌ or both at the time the action contained in the verb takes place.

e.g.	جَاءَ زَيْدٌ رَاكِبًا	Zayd came while mounted/riding.
	جِئْتُ زَيْدًا نَائِمًا	I came to Zayd while he was sleeping.
	كَلَّمْتُ زَيْدًا جَالِسَيْنِ	I spoke to Zayd while both of us were sitting.

Notes:

1. The condition itself is known as حَالٌ, whereas the one whose condition is being described is known as ذُو الْحَالِ.

2. The حَالٌ gets a نَصْبٌ, which is generally in the form of two *fathahs*.

3. The ذُو الْحَالِ is generally مَعْرِفَةٌ and the حَالٌ is generally نَكِرَةٌ.

    e.g. جَاءَ زَيْدٌ رَاكِبًا   Zayd came riding/while he was mounted.

4. If the ذُو الْحَالِ is نَكِرَةٌ, the حَالٌ is brought before the ذُو الْحَالِ.

    e.g. جَاءَنِيْ رَاكِبًا رَجُلٌ   A man came to me riding/while he was mounted.

5. The ذُو الْحَالِ can be a ضَمِيْرٌ.

    e.g. زَيْدٌ أَكَلَ جَالِسًا   Zayd ate sitting.

    Here, the ذُو الْحَالِ is هُوَ, which is the hidden ضَمِيْرٌ in أَكَلَ.

6. The حَالٌ can be a sentence.

    - If the حَالٌ is a جُمْلَةٌ اِسْمِيَّةٌ, then a وَاوٌ (with or without a ضَمِيْرٌ) is added to give the meaning of condition.
      e.g. لَا تَقْرَبُوا الصَّلَوةَ وَأَنْتُمْ سُكْرَى   Don't come near *salah* while you are intoxicated.

    - If the حَالٌ is a جُمْلَةٌ فِعْلِيَّةٌ and the فِعْلٌ is فِعْلُ الْمَاضِيْ, قَدْ has to appear before the الْفِعْلُ الْمَاضِيْ.
      e.g. جَاءَ زَيْدٌ وَقَدْ خَرَجَ خَادِمُهُ   Zayd came while his servant had left.

---

[48] For more details, examples and exercises, please refer to *al-Nahw al-Wadih, Ibtida'iyyah*, vol. 3, 101-109.

Sentence Analysis:

1. جَاءَ زَيْدٌ رَاكِبًا — Zayd came riding/while he was mounted.

رَاكِبًا	زَيْدٌ	جَاءَ
حَالٌ	ذُو الْحَالِ	
جُمْلَةٌ فِعْلِيَّةٌ خَبَرِيَّةٌ = فَاعِلٌ + فِعْلٌ		

2. جِئْتُ عَمْرًا نَائِمًا — I came to 'Amr while he was asleep.

نَائِمًا	عَمْرًا	جِئْتُ
حَالٌ	ذُو الْحَالِ	
جُمْلَةٌ فِعْلِيَّةٌ خَبَرِيَّةٌ = مَفْعُولٌ بِهِ + فِعْلٌ + فَاعِلٌ		

3. لَقِيتُ بَكْرًا وَهُوَ جَالِسٌ — I met Bakr while he was sitting.

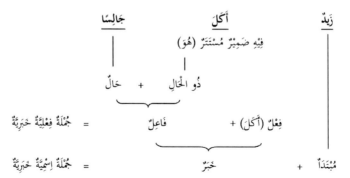

4. زَيْدٌ أَكَلَ جَالِسًا — Zayd ate while sitting.

جَالِسًا	أَكَلَ	زَيْدٌ
	فِيهِ ضَمِيرٌ مُسْتَتِرٌ (هُوَ)	
حَالٌ	ذُو الْحَالِ	
جُمْلَةٌ فِعْلِيَّةٌ خَبَرِيَّةٌ = فَاعِلٌ + فِعْلٌ (أَكَلَ)		
جُمْلَةٌ اسْمِيَّةٌ خَبَرِيَّةٌ = خَبَرٌ + مُبْتَدَأٌ		

EXERCISE

1. Translate, fill in the *i'raab* and point out the حَالّ and ذُو الحَالِ in the following sentences.

i.	أحب التلميذ مجتهدا	vi.	لا تأكلوا الطعام حارا
ii.	لقيت زيدا راكبين	vii.	نصرت زيدا مشدودا
iii.	لا تأكلوا الفاكهة وهي فجة	viii.	غاب أخوك وقد حضر جميع أصدقاءه
iv.	رجع القائد منصورا	ix.	دخل اللص المنزل وأهله نائمون
v.	قطف التاجر العنب ناضجا	x.	نمت الأشجار ولما يثمر

Section 3.8.7

تَمْيِيز / تَمْيِيز

Definition: It is an اسْمٌ نَكِرَةٌ, which removes the ambiguity or vagueness created by the previous noun. This ambiguity may be in distance, weight, measure, number, etc.

    e.g.   رَأَيْتُ أَحَدَ عَشَرَ كَوْكَبًا   I saw eleven stars.

    Here, the word (كَوْكَبًا) clarifies what (أَحَدَ عَشَرَ) refers to.

Sentence Analysis:

رَأَيْتُ	أَحَدَ عَشَرَ	كَوْكَبًا
	مُمَيَّزٌ +	تَمْيِيزٌ
فِعْلٌ + فَاعِلٌ	+	مَفْعُولٌ بِهِ	= جُمْلَةٌ فِعْلِيَّةٌ خَبَرِيَّةٌ

Notes:

- The ambiguous noun is called مُمَيَّزٌ and the noun which clarifies it is called تَمْيِيزٌ or مُمَيِّزٌ.
- The تَمْيِيزٌ is *mansoob* and gets two *fathahs*.
- Sometimes, the مُمَيَّزٌ is not mentioned in words but is understood from the meaning of the sentence (مَلْحُوظٌ).

    e.g.   حَسُنَ الْوَلَدُ كَلَامًا   The boy is good in terms of (his) speech.

- If the مُمَيَّزٌ is a number, the rules with regards to the usage of numerals (on the next page) must be kept in mind.

EXERCISE

1. Translate, fill in the *i'raab* and point out the مُمَيَّزٌ and تَمْيِيزٌ in the following sentences.

i.	فى الحقل عشرون بقرة		v.	طاب المكان هواء
ii.	بعته ذراعا حريرا		vi.	لا أملك شبرا أرضا
iii.	الفيل أكبر من الجمل جسما		vii.	شربت رطلا لبنا
iv.	أطعمت الدجاجة ملء الكف حبا		viii.	شربت كوبا ماء

---

[49] For more details, examples and exercises, please refer to *al-Nahw al-Wadih, Ibtida'iyyah*, vol. 3, 110-119.

Rules for أَسْمَاءُ الْعَدَدِ (Numerals)

Before we proceed, it should be pointed out that

عَدَدٌ (number) is the مُمَيِّزٌ and مَعْدُودٌ (the counted noun) is the تَمْيِيزٌ.

One and two (1-2)

- The مَعْدُودٌ will appear first and the عَدَدٌ will appear second.
- The عَدَدٌ and the مَعْدُودٌ must correspond in all aspects.

    e.g.   وَلَدٌ وَاحِدٌ   one boy

    بِنْتٌ وَاحِدَةٌ   one girl

    Note: Normally, for one or two boy, girl, men etc., one would simply say وَلَدٌ or وَلَدَانِ, etc. However, at times, the number is used for emphasis.

Three through Ten (3-10)

- From three onwards, the عَدَدٌ will appear first and the مَعْدُودٌ second.
- The مَعْدُودٌ will be جَمْعٌ مَجْرُورٌ.
- The عَدَدٌ and the مَعْدُودٌ must be of opposite gender.

    e.g.   ثَلَاثَةُ أَقْلَامٍ   three pens

    خَمْسُ سَيَّارَاتٍ   five cars

    Note: In choosing the correct عَدَدٌ gender, the singular form of the مَعْدُودٌ will be taken into account.

    e.g.   سَبْعُ لَيَالٍ وَثَمَانِيَةُ أَيَّامٍ   seven nights and eight days

    Here, the singular لَيْلَةٌ (night) of لَيَالٍ is feminine, and يَوْمٌ (day) of أَيَّامٌ is masculine.

- For ten, the masculine form is عَشْرٌ, and the feminine form is عَشَرَةٌ.

Eleven and Twelve (11-12)

- From eleven onwards till 99, the مَعْدُودٌ will be وَاحِدٌ مَنْصُوبٌ.
- The عَدَدٌ and the مَعْدُودٌ must have the same gender.

    e.g.   أَحَدَ عَشَرَ كَوْكَبًا   eleven stars

    اِثْنَتَا عَشْرَةَ بِنْتًا   twelve girls

- From 11–19, the ش of عشر/عشرة will get a *fathah* when used with a masculine and a *sukoon* when used with a feminine.[50]

---

[50] For feminine, the form عَشِرَةٌ is also used. See W. Wright, *Arabic Grammar*, (Mineola, NY: Dover Publications, 2005), Part 1, 256. Also see *Sharh ibn 'Aqil*, vol. 4, 71.

Thirteen through Nineteen (13-19)

- The مَعْدُود will be مَنْصُوبٌ وَاحِدٌ.
- The gender of the first part of the عَدَد should be opposite of the gender of the مَعْدُود.
  - e.g.   أَرْبَعَةَ عَشَرَ رَجُلًا   fourteen men
  - تِسْعَ عَشْرَةَ بِنْتًا   nineteen girls
- The "ten" عَشَر (masc.)/عَشْرَة (fem.) will agree with the مَعْدُود in terms of gender.

Twenty till Ninety (20, 30, 40,…,90)

- The مَعْدُود will be مَنْصُوبٌ وَاحِدٌ.
- The gender of عِشْرُونَ to تِسْعُونَ (20,30,40,…90) will remain the same, irrespective of whether the مَعْدُود is masculine or feminine.
  - e.g.   عِشْرُونَ رَجُلًا   twenty men
  - ثَلَاثُونَ بِنْتًا   thirty girls

Twenty-one and Twenty-two (21-22)

- The مَعْدُود will be مَنْصُوبٌ وَاحِدٌ.
- The first part of the عَدَد and the مَعْدُود must have the same gender.
  - e.g.   وَاحِدٌ وَعِشْرُونَ رَجُلًا   twenty-one men
  - إِحْدَى وَعِشْرُونَ بِنْتًا   twenty-one girls
- The same will apply to 31-32, 41-42…91-92.

Twenty-three through Twenty-nine (23-29)

- The مَعْدُود will be مَنْصُوبٌ وَاحِدٌ.
- The gender of the first part of the عَدَد should be opposite of the gender of the مَعْدُود.
  - e.g.   أَرْبَعَةٌ وَعِشْرُونَ رَجُلًا   twenty-four men
  - سِتٌّ وَعِشْرُونَ بِنْتًا   twenty-six girls
- The same will apply to 33-39, 43-49…93-99.
- The "tens" will remain the same, irrespective of whether the مَعْدُود is masculine or feminine.

Hundred (100)

- The مَعْدُوْدٌ will be وَاحِدٌ مَجْرُوْرٌ.
- مِائَة will remain the same, irrespective of whether the مَعْدُوْدٌ is masculine or feminine.

  e.g.   مِائَةُ رَجُلٍ   hundred men   مِائَةُ بِنْتٍ   hundred girls

- For 200, مِائَتَا will be used. (حَالَةُ النَّصْبِ وَ الْجَرِّ in مِائَتَيْ)

  e.g.   مِائَتَا بِنْتٍ   two hundred girls

  مِائَتَيْ بِنْتٍ   two hundred girls

- Since مِائَة is feminine, the number **before** مِائَة will be masculine.

  e.g.   أَرْبَعُمِائَةِ رَجُلٍ   four hundred men

  أَرْبَعُمِائَةِ بِنْتٍ   four hundred women

- If there are units and tens with the 100's as well, their respective gender rules will apply.

  e.g.   مِائَةٌ وَعَشَرَةُ كُتُبٍ   hundred and ten books

  مِائَةٌ وَخَمْسٌ وَأَرْبَعُوْنَ كُرَّاسَةً   hundred and forty-five note-books

Thousand (1,000)

- The مَعْدُوْدٌ will be وَاحِدٌ مَجْرُوْرٌ.
- أَلْفٌ will remain the same, irrespective of whether the مَعْدُوْدٌ is masculine or feminine.

  e.g.   أَلْفُ رَجُلٍ   thousand men   أَلْفُ بِنْتٍ   thousand girls

- Since أَلْفٌ is masculine, the number **before** أَلْفٌ will be feminine.

  e.g.   أَرْبَعَةُ آلَافِ رَجُلٍ   four thousand men

  أَرْبَعَةُ آلَافِ بِنْتٍ   four thousand women

  Note: The plural for أَلْفٌ is آلَافٌ.

Million (1,000,000)

- The مَعْدُوْدٌ will be وَاحِدٌ مَجْرُوْرٌ.
- مِلْيُوْنٌ will remain the same, irrespective of whether the مَعْدُوْدٌ is masculine or feminine.

  e.g.   مِلْيُوْنُ رَجُلٍ   million men

  مِلْيُوْنُ بِنْتٍ   million girls

- Since مِلْيُوْنٌ is masculine, the number **before** مِلْيُوْنٌ will be feminine.

  e.g.   أَرْبَعَةُ مَلَايِيْنَ رَجُلٍ   four million men

  أَرْبَعَةُ مَلَايِيْنَ امْرَأَةٍ   four million women

  Note: The plural for مِلْيُوْنٌ is مَلَايِيْنُ.

EXERCISES

1. Write the following in Arabic.

    i. 2 schools
    ii. 12 women
    iii. 17 doors
    iv. 21 cars
    v. 150 houses
    vi. 444 miles
    vii. 11 books
    viii. 14 chairs
    ix. 26 boys
    x. 111 elephants
    xi. 195 keys
    xii. 3,333 roses

2. Translate the following sentences and fill in the *i'raab*.

    i. في البستان تسع وتسعون نخلة
    ii. مساحة الدار ألفا ذراع
    iii. للحجرة ثلاث شبابيك
    iv. باع التاجر أربعة عشر قنطارا قطنا
    v. في الكتاب أربع وعشرون صفحة
    vi. في السنة اثنا عشر شهرا
    vii. عمر أخيك الآن خمس وثلاثون سنة
    viii. باضت الدجاجة ثلاث بيضات

Section 3.8.8[51]

مُسْتَثْنًى

اِسْتِثْنَاءٌ means to exclude.

مُسْتَثْنًى is that noun, which has been excluded and appears after the حَرْفُ الْإِسْتِثْنَاءِ.

مُسْتَثْنًى مِنْهُ is that noun from which the مُسْتَثْنَى has been excluded. It appears before حَرْفُ الْإِسْتِثْنَاءِ.

حُرُوفُ الْإِسْتِثْنَاءِ are as follows:

إِلَّا   غَيْرَ   سِوَى   حَاشَا   خَلَا   عَدَا   مَا خَلَا   مَا عَدَا

e.g.   جَاءَ الْقَوْمُ إِلَّا زَيْدًا   The people came except Zayd.

جَاءَ		الْقَوْمُ	+	إِلَّا	+	زَيْدًا
فِعْلٌ	+	فَاعِلٌ		حَرْفُ الْإِسْتِثْنَاءِ	+	مُسْتَثْنًى
				مُسْتَثْنًى مِنْهُ		
		= جُمْلَةٌ فِعْلِيَّةٌ خَبَرِيَّةٌ				

Related Terminology

مُسْتَثْنًى مُتَّصِلٌ refers to the case when the مُسْتَثْنَى was included in the مُسْتَثْنَى مِنْهُ before the اِسْتِثْنَاءُ.

e.g. جَاءَ الْقَوْمُ إِلَّا زَيْدًا   The people came except Zayd.
(Zayd was one of the people before the exclusion.)

مُسْتَثْنًى مُنْقَطِعٌ refers to the case when the مُسْتَثْنَى was not included in the مُسْتَثْنَى مِنْهُ before the اِسْتِثْنَاءُ.

e.g. سَجَدَ الْمَلَائِكَةُ إِلَّا إِبْلِيسَ   The angels prostrated except Iblees.
(Iblees was never one of the angels.)

جَاءَ الْقَوْمُ إِلَّا حِمَارًا   The people came except a donkey.
(Donkey was never included among the people.)

مُسْتَثْنًى مُفَرَّغٌ refers to that sentence in which the مُسْتَثْنَى مِنْهُ is not mentioned.

e.g. مَا جَاءَ إِلَّا زَيْدٌ   No one came except Zayd.

مُسْتَثْنًى غَيْرُ مُفَرَّغٍ refers to that sentence in which the مُسْتَثْنَى مِنْهُ is mentioned.

e.g. جَاءَ الْقَوْمُ إِلَّا زَيْدًا   The people came except Zayd.

---

[51] For more details, examples and exercises, please refer to *al-Nahw al-Wadih, Ibtida'iyyah*, vol. 3, 88-100.

كَلَامٌ مُثْبَتٌ / كَلَامٌ مُوجَبٌ (positive statement) refers to that sentence, which does not have a نَفْيٌ, اِسْتِفْهَامٌ or نَهْيٌ.

e.g. جَاءَ الْقَوْمُ إِلَّا زَيْدًا The people came except Zayd.

كَلَامٌ مَنْفِيٌّ / كَلَامٌ غَيْرُ مُوجَبٍ (negative sentence) refers to that sentence, which does have a نَفْيٌ, نَهْيٌ or اِسْتِفْهَامٌ.

e.g. مَا جَاءَ الْقَوْمُ إِلَّا زَيْدًا The people did not come except Zayd.

The i'raab of the various types of مُسْتَثْنَى are as given below:

Table 3.8
إِعْرَابُ الْمُسْتَثْنَى

حُرُوفُ الْاِسْتِثْنَاءِ	Sentence Type			إِعْرَابُ الْمُسْتَثْنَى	Example
1. إِلَّا	مُنْقَطِعٌ			مَنْصُوبٌ	سَجَدَ الْمَلَائِكَةُ إِلَّا إِبْلِيسَ The angels prostrated except Iblees.
2. إِلَّا	مُتَّصِلٌ	مُوجَبٌ		مَنْصُوبٌ	جَاءَنِي الْقَوْمُ إِلَّا زَيْدًا The people came to me except zayd.
3. إِلَّا	مُتَّصِلٌ	غَيْرُ مُوجَبٍ	غَيْرُ مُفَرَّغٍ	مَنْصُوبٌ – or – same as مُسْتَثْنَى مِنْهُ	مَا جَاءَنِي أَحَدٌ إِلَّا زَيْدًا مَا جَاءَنِي أَحَدٌ إِلَّا زَيْدٌ No one came to me except Zayd.
4. إِلَّا	مُتَّصِلٌ	غَيْرُ مُوجَبٍ	مُفَرَّغٌ	according to the عَامِلٌ governing إِلَّا (as if مُسْتَثْنَى مِنْهُ does not exist)	مَا جَاءَ إِلَّا زَيْدٌ No one came except Zayd. مَا رَأَيْتُ إِلَّا زَيْدًا I did not see anyone except Zayd. مَا مَرَرْتُ إِلَّا بِزَيْدٍ I did not pass by anyone except Zayd.
5. مَا خَلَا – مَا عَدَا	All types			مَنْصُوبٌ	جَاءَ الْقَوْمُ مَا خَلَا زَيْدًا جَاءَ الْقَوْمُ مَا عَدَا زَيْدًا The people came except Zayd.

Table 3.8 – *Continued*

حُرُوْفُ الْاِسْتِثْنَاءِ	Sentence Type	إِعْرَابُ الْمُسْتَثْنَى	Example
6. خَلَا – عَدَا – حَاشَا	All types	مَنْصُوْبٌ – or – مَجْرُوْرٌ (as a preposition)	جَاءَ الْقَوْمُ خَلَا/عَدَا/حَاشَا زَيْدًا جَاءَ الْقَوْمُ خَلَا/عَدَا/حَاشَا زَيْدٍ The people came except Zayd.
7. غَيْر – سِوَى	All types	مَجْرُوْرٌ	جَاءَ الْقَوْمُ غَيْرَ زَيْدٍ جَاءَ الْقَوْمُ سِوَى زَيْدٍ The people came except Zayd.

Note: The *i'raab* of the word غَيْر is the same as that of إِلَّا بِ مُسْتَثْنَى. Thus, the simple way to determine the *i'raab* of غَيْر is to replace غَيْر with إِلَّا. Now, whatever *i'raab* مُسْتَثْنَى was supposed to get, should be given to غَيْر.

For example, we have two sentences, 1) جَاءَ الْقَوْمُ غَيْرَ زَيْدٍ and 2) مَا جَاءَ غَيْرُ زَيْدٍ.

To determine the *i'raab* of غَيْر, follow the following two steps for each of these sentences.

    a. Replace غير with إِلَّا and see what the *i'raab* of the مُسْتَثْنَى would be.

        2) مَا جَاءَ إِلَّا زَيْدٌ   1) جَاءَ الْقَوْمُ إِلَّا زَيْدًا

        The first sentence is مُوْجَبٌ, so the مُسْتَثْنَى will be *mansoob*. The second sentence is غَيْرُ مُوْجَبٍ and مُفَرَّغٌ, so the مُسْتَثْنَى is according to the *'aamil*. Thus, it will be *marfoo'*.

    b. The *i'raab* of the مُسْتَثْنَى (with إِلَّا) will be given to غَيْر.

        2) مَا جَاءَ غَيْرُ زَيْدٍ   1) جَاءَ الْقَوْمُ غَيْرَ زَيْدٍ

EXERCISES

1. Translate, fill in the *i'raab* and explain the *i'raab* of the *mustathnaa*.

    i. رأيت الجنود إلا القائد   v. دخلت غرف البيت خلا غرفة النوم

    ii. صام الغلام رمضان غير يوم   vi. ما عاد المريض عائد غير الطبيب

    iii. زرت مساجد المدينة ما خلا واحدا   vii. قرأت الكتاب إلا صفحتين

    iv. جاء القوم إلا حمارا   viii. ما جاء إلا معلم

Section 3.9[52]

اَلْمَجْرُوْرَاتُ – Words Which Are Always *Majroor*

There are two types of words that are always *majroor*. These are as follows:

1. Noun preceded by a حَرْفُ جَرٍّ.

    e.g.   فِي الْكِتَابِ   in the book

2. مُضَافٌ إِلَيْهِ

    e.g.   كِتَابُ زَيْدٍ   book of Zayd

---

[52] For more examples and exercises, please refer to *al-Nahw al-Wadih, Ibtida'iyyah*, vol. 1, 76-81.

Section 3.10
اَلتَّوَابِعُ

Definition: A تَابِعٌ is that noun, which follows the noun before it in terms of *i'raab* (and some other things which vary from تَابِعٌ to تَابِعٌ). The preceding noun is called the مَتْبُوعٌ.

- The عَامِلٌ which governs the مَتْبُوعٌ also governs the تَابِعٌ.
- There are five تَوَابِعُ:

  1) اَلنَّعْتُ/اَلصِّفَةُ   2) اَلتَّأْكِيدُ/اَلتَّوْكِيدُ   3) اَلْبَدَلُ
  4) اَلْعَطْفُ بِحَرْفٍ/عَطْفُ النَّسَقِ   5) عَطْفُ الْبَيَانِ

Section 3.10.1[53]
اَلنَّعْتُ أَوِ اَلصِّفَةُ – Adjective[54]

اَلنَّعْتُ/اَلصِّفَةُ is of two types: 1) نَعْتٌ حَقِيقِيٌّ   2) نَعْتٌ سَبَبِيٌّ

1. نَعْتٌ حَقِيقِيٌّ: It is that word, which describes the actual مَتْبُوعٌ.
   - As mentioned in section 1.4.3, the نَعْتٌ follows the مَنْعُوتٌ, which is the مَتْبُوعٌ in this case, in the following:
     a. *I'raab*   b. Gender
     c. Being *ma'rifah* or *nakirah*   d. Being singular, dual or plural
   - The نَعْتٌ can be a complete sentence, in which case the مَنْعُوتٌ must be نَكِرَةٌ.
   - The نَعْتٌ, which is a sentence must have a ضَمِيرٌ which refers to the نَكِرَةٌ مَنْعُوتٌ.
     e.g. جَاءَنِي وَلَدٌ يَرْكَبُ الدَّرَّاجَةَ   A boy who was riding the bicycle came to me.

---

[53] For more details, examples and exercises, please refer to *al-Nahw al-Wadih*, *Ibtida'iyyah*, vol. 3, 134-142.
[54] نَعْتٌ is another name for صِفَةٌ; and مَنْعُوتٌ is another name for مَوْصُوفٌ.

Note:

- If a مَعْرِفَة is followed by a sentence, it will be a خَبَر or حَال.

    Example 1   اَلْوَلَدُ يَرْكَبُ الدَّرَّاجَةَ   The boy is riding the bicycle.

    Here, (اَلْوَلَدُ) is مُبْتَدَأٌ, and (يَرْكَبُ الدَّرَّاجَةَ) is the خَبَر.

    Example 2   جَاءَنِي الْوَلَدُ يَرْكَبُ الدَّرَّاجَةَ

    The boy came to me while riding the bicycle.

    Here, (اَلْوَلَدُ) is ذُو الْحَال, and (يَرْكَبُ الدَّرَّاجَةَ) is the حَال.

Sentence Analysis

1. جَاءَ رَجُلٌ عَالِمٌ   A learned man came.

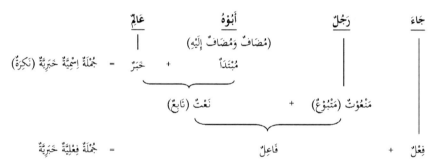

2. جَاءَ رَجُلٌ أَبُوهُ عَالِمٌ   A man whose father is learned, came.

2. نَعْتٌ سَبَبِيٌّ: It is that word, which does not describe the مَنْعُوتٌ, but describes that which is connected to the مَنْعُوتٌ.

   e.g.   جَاءَنِي وَلَدٌ عَالِمٌ أَبُوهُ   A boy whose father is learned, came to me.

   Here, عَالِمٌ is describing أَبُوهُ, which is connected to the مَنْعُوتٌ (وَلَدٌ). In other words, it is describing the مَنْعُوتٌ indirectly.

Notes:

1. In نَعْتٌ سَبَبِيٌّ, the مَنْعُوتٌ and نَعْتٌ must correspond in only two aspects:
   a. I'raab
   b. Being *ma'rifah* or *nakirah*

2. The نَعْتْ will always be singular, irrespective of whether the مَنْعُوتْ is singular, dual or plural.

   e.g. هَاتَانِ صُورَتَانِ جَمِيْلٌ إِطَارَاهُمَا   These are two pictures whose frames are beautiful.

3. The نَعْتْ will correspond in gender to the word **after it**.

   e.g. جَاءَتِ السَّيِّدَةُ الْعَاقِلُ وَلَدُهَا   The lady, whose son is intelligent, came.

Sentence Analysis:

1. جَاءَتْ امْرَأَةٌ عَالِمٌ ابْنُهَا   A woman whose son is learned, came.

جَاءَتْ	امْرَأَةٌ	عَالِمٌ	ابْنُهَا
		اِسْمُ الْفَاعِلِ + فَاعِلٌ	(مُضَافٌ وَمُضَافٌ إِلَيْهِ) — جُمْلَةٌ فِعْلِيَّةٌ خَبَرِيَّةٌ
	مَنْعُوتٌ (مَتْبُوعٌ) + نَعْتٌ (تَابِعٌ)		
فِعْلٌ + فَاعِلٌ			— جُمْلَةٌ فِعْلِيَّةٌ خَبَرِيَّةٌ

Note: In this example, عَالِمٌ is the نَعْتْ سَبَبِيٌّ of امْرَأَةٌ. Because of امْرَأَةٌ, it is *marfoo'* and نَكِرَةٌ. However, it follows ابْنُهَا, or more precisely ابْنُ, in being masculine.[55]

EXERCISE

1. Translate, fill in the *i'raab* and point out the نَعْتٌ حَقِيْقِيٌّ and the نَعْتٌ سَبَبِيٌّ in the following sentences.

   i. ركبت الحصان الجميل سرجه
   ii. هو رجل عالمة ابنته
   iii. هؤلاء بنات عاقلات
   iv. شاهدنا قطارا سيره سريع
   v. أوقدت مصباحا نوره قوي
   vi. هذا عمل ينفع
   vii. هذا منزل ضيق
   viii. جاء الرجل المهذب أخوه

---

[55] There seems to be a contradiction between the sentence analysis and the note given above for نَعْتٌ سَبَبِيٌّ. All the books of *Nahw* that we referred to, including *'Ilm al-Nahw*, *al-Nahw al-Wadih*, and *Sharh ibn 'Aqil*, agree that in this example, only عَالِمٌ is the نَعْتٌ سَبَبِيٌّ. Yet, in *'Ilm al-Nahw*, the author, Mawlana Charthawali, after explaining the rules for نَعْتٌ سَبَبِيٌّ, has given this example of sentence analysis, in which he makes عَالِمٌ ابْنُهَا the نَعْتٌ of امْرَأَةٌ. This suggests that there can be two ways of looking at this.

2. Analyze the following sentences and and point out the difference between them.

   i. هذا الولد ضاحك   iii. جاء الولد ضاحكا
   ii. هذا ولد ضاحك

Section 3.10.2[56]
اَلتَّوْكِيدُ / اَلتَّأْكِيدُ – Emphasis

Definition: It is that تَابِعٌ, which gives emphasis to the مَتْبُوعٌ in the matter related to it or emphasizes the inclusion of all members of the مَتْبُوعٌ in the matter related to it.

e.g. جَاءَنِي زَيْدٌ زَيْدٌ (The second 'Zayd' emphasized Zayd's coming.)

جَاءَ الْقَوْمُ كُلُّهُمْ (كُلُّهُمْ emphasized that all came, no one remained.)

- The تَابِعٌ is called تَأْكِيدٌ and the مَتْبُوعٌ is called مُؤَكَّدٌ.

There are two types of تَأْكِيدٌ: لَفْظِيٌّ and مَعْنَوِيٌّ

1. اَلتَّوْكِيدُ اللَّفْظِيُّ – Verbal Emphasis: The emphasis is attained by repeating the مُؤَكَّدٌ, which may be ضَمِيرٌ, حَرْفٌ, فِعْلٌ, اِسْمٌ, or sentence.

    e.g.
جَاءَ زَيْدٌ زَيْدٌ	Zayd definitely came.
حَضَرَ حَضَرَ الْغَائِبُ	The absent one definitely became present.
لَا لَا أَخُونُ الْعَهْدَ	I will definitely not break the pledge.
اِفْتَحْ أَنْتَ النَّافِذَةَ	*You* open the window.
أَنْتَ الْمَلُومُ أَنْتَ الْمَلُومُ	You are, indeed, the censured one.

2. اَلتَّوْكِيدُ الْمَعْنَوِيُّ – Emphasis Through Meaning: The emphasis is attained with any of the following words:

    نَفْسٌ عَيْنٌ كِلَا كِلْتَا كُلٌّ أَجْمَعُ أَكْتَعُ أَبْصَعُ أَبْتَعُ

    Below, we discuss each of these.

    a. عَيْنٌ، نَفْسٌ (himself, herself, itself)
    - These are used for singular, dual and plural.
    - They have to be مُضَافٌ to a ضَمِيرٌ.
    - Their ضَمِيرٌ must agree with the مُؤَكَّدٌ in terms of gender and singularity (or duality/plurality), while the form (صِيغَةٌ) should agree with the مُؤَكَّدٌ in terms of singularity (or duality/plurality). The exception is that the plural form (صِيغَةٌ) of نَفْسٌ and عَيْنٌ is used in place of the dual form.

        e.g.
قَامَ زَيْدٌ نَفْسُهُ/عَيْنُهُ	Zayd himself stood.
قَامَ الزَّيْدَانِ أَنْفُسُهُمَا/أَعْيُنُهُمَا	The two Zayds themselves stood.
قَامَ الزَّيْدُونَ أَنْفُسُهُمْ/أَعْيُنُهُمْ	The (many) Zayds themselves stood.

---

[56] For more details, examples and exercises, please refer to *al-Nahw al-Wadih, Ibtida'iyyah*, vol. 3, 143-152

جَاءَتِ الْمُعَلِّمَةُ عَيْنُهَا/نَفْسُهَا	The female teacher herself came.
جَاءَتِ الْمُعَلِّمَتَانِ أَعْيُنُهُمَا/أَنْفُسُهُمَا	The two female teachers themselves came.
جَاءَتِ الْمُعَلِّمَاتُ أَعْيُنُهُنَّ/أَنْفُسُهُنَّ	The (many) female teachers themselves came.

b. كِلْتَا، كِلَا (both)

- These are used for dual only.
- كِلَا is masculine and كِلْتَا is feminine.
- It must be مُضَافٌ to a dual ضَمِيرٌ.

  e.g.

قَامَ الرَّجُلَانِ كِلَاهُمَا	Both of the men stood up.
قَامَتِ الْمُعَلِّمَتَانِ كِلْتَاهُمَا	Both of the female teachers stood up.

c. جَمِيعٌ، أَجْمَعُ، كُلٌّ (all)

- They are used for singular and plural.
- كُلٌّ and جَمِيعٌ should be مُضَافٌ to a ضَمِيرٌ, which must correspond to the مُؤَكَّد.
- أَجْمَعُ is used with its form (صِيغَة) changing to correspond to the مُؤَكَّد.

  e.g.

قَرَأْتُ الْكِتَابَ كُلَّهُ	I read the whole book.
جَاءَ الرِّجَالُ كُلُّهُمْ	All the men came.
جَاءَ الرِّجَالُ جَمِيعُهُمْ	All the men came.
جَاءَ النَّاسُ أَجْمَعُونَ	All the people came.

Note: كُلٌّ, جَمِيعٌ and أَجْمَعُ can only be used for emphasis in those things, which have parts or can be divided. Thus, أَكْرَمْتُ زَيْدًا كُلَّهُ (I treated all of Zayd hospitably) would be incorrect.

d. أَبْتَعُ، أَبْصَعُ، أَكْتَعُ

- These are used for greater emphasis.
- They appear after أَجْمَعُ. They are not used without أَجْمَعُ nor can they appear before أَجْمَعُ.

  e.g.

جَاءَ الْقَوْمُ أَجْمَعُونَ أَكْتَعُونَ/أَبْتَعُونَ/أَبْصَعُونَ	All of the people came.
قَامَتِ النِّسَاءُ جُمَعُ كُتَعُ/بُتَعُ/بُصَعُ	All of the women stood up.

Sentence Analysis

جَاءَ الْقَوْمُ كُلُّهُمْ أَجْمَعُونَ   All the people came.

EXERCISE

1. Translate, fill in the *i'raab* and analyze the following sentences.

i.	قابلت الوزير نفسه	vi.	رأيت التمساح التمساح
ii.	ذبحنا الكبشين كليهما	vii.	قطعنا نحن أنفسنا الطريق كله
iii.	سجد الملئكة كلهم أجمعون إلا ابليس	viii.	الملك كله لله
iv.	إياك إياك النميمة	ix.	غربت غربت الشمس
v.	عاد القائد عينه	x.	حذار حذار من الإهمال

Section 3.10.3[57]
اَلْبَدَلُ – Substitute

Definition: A بَدَلٌ is that تَابِعٌ, which is actually intended in the sentence and not its مَتْبُوعٌ. The مَتْبُوعٌ merely serves as an introduction to the تَابِعُ.

- The تَابِعُ is called بَدَلٌ (substitute) and the مَتْبُوعٌ is called مُبْدَلٌ مِنْهُ or مُبْدَلٌ مِنْهُ (the substituted).

  e.g.   جَاءَ زَيْدٌ أَخُوكَ   Zayd, your brother, came.

There are four types of بَدَل:

1) بَدَلُ كُلٍّ مِنْ كُلٍّ   (2 بَدَلُ بَعْضٍ مِنْ كُلٍّ   (3 بَدَلُ الْاِشْتِمَالِ   (4 بَدَلُ الْغَلَطِ

1. بَدَلُ كُلٍّ مِنْ كُلٍّ (also called بَدَلُ الْكُلِّ): It is that بَدَلٌ, which refers to the exact same thing as the مُبْدَلُ مِنْهُ.

   e.g.   جَاءَ زَيْدٌ أَخُوكَ   Zayd, your brother, came.

2. بَدَلُ بَعْضٍ مِنْ كُلٍّ (also called بَدَلُ الْبَعْضِ): It is that بَدَلٌ, which refers to a **part** of the مُبْدَلُ مِنْهُ.
   - The بَدَلٌ must have a ضَمِيرٌ, which refers to the مُبْدَلُ مِنْهُ.

   e.g.   ضَرَبْتُ زَيْدًا رَأْسَهُ   I hit Zayd's head.

3. بَدَلُ الْاِشْتِمَالِ: It is that بَدَلٌ, which is related to the مُبْدَلُ مِنْهُ, but is not part of it.
   - The بَدَلٌ must have a ضَمِيرٌ, which refers to the مُبْدَلُ مِنْهُ.

   e.g.   سُرِقَ زَيْدٌ قَمِيصُهُ   Zayd's shirt was stolen.

4. بَدَلُ الْغَلَطِ: It is that بَدَلٌ, which is mentioned **after an error**, as a correction.

   e.g.   اِشْتَرَيْتُ فَرَسًا حِمَارًا   I bought a horse; no, a donkey.

---

[57] For more details, examples and exercises, please refer to *al-Nahw al-Wadih, Ibtida'iyyah*, vol. 3, 163-167.

EXERCISE

1. Translate, fill in the *i'raab* and analyze the following sentences.

    i. قضيت الدين ثلثه
    ii. سرني الخادم أمانته
    iii. ذهب السياح أكثرهم إلى الوادي
    iv. سطع القمر نوره
    v. سرتنا الشوارع نظافتها
    vi. قدم الأمير الوزير
    vii. عاملت التاجر زيدا
    viii. تمزق الكتاب غلافه
    ix. أغلقت عائشة البستان بابه
    x. كان أبو حامد الغزالي مجددا

Section 3.10.4

اَلْعَطْفُ بِحَرْفٍ/عَطْفُ النَّسَقِ – Conjunction

Definition: It is that تَابِعٌ, which appears after a حَرْفُ عَطْفٍ. The حَرْفُ عَطْفٍ appears between the تَابِعٌ and the مَتْبُوعٌ. The meaning of the عَامِلٌ applicable to the مَتْبُوعٌ is also applicable to the تَابِعٌ.

- The تَابِعٌ is called مَعْطُوفٌ and the مَتْبُوعٌ is called مَعْطُوفٌ عَلَيْهِ.

    e.g. جَاءَ زَيْدٌ وَعَمْرٌو   Zayd and 'Amr came.

حُرُوفُ الْعَطْفِ:

The various حُرُوفُ عَطْفٍ are as follows:

لٰكِنْ   بَلْ   لَا   أَمْ   أَوْ   إِمَّا   حَتَّى   ثُمَّ   فَ   وَ

Their details are as follows:

وَ (and): This is without regard to sequence.

   e.g. جَاءَ زَيْدٌ وَبَكْرٌ   Zayd and Bakr came.
   Here, sequence is not considered.

فَ (then, thus):

- It shows sequence.
   e.g. جَاءَ زَيْدٌ فَبَكْرٌ   Zayd came. Then, Bakr (came).

- It can also show cause (سَبَبٌ).
   e.g. أَنْزَلَ مِنَ السَّمَاءِ مَاءً فَتُصْبِحُ الْأَرْضُ مُخْضَرَّةً
   He sends down water from the sky. Therefore, the earth becomes green.

ثُمَّ (then): It shows sequence with delay.

   e.g. جَاءَ زَيْدٌ ثُمَّ بَكْرٌ   Zayd came. Then, (after some time) Bakr (came).

حَتَّى (upto, till, even): It shows the end point (غَايَةٌ).

   e.g. قَرَأْتُ الْقُرْآنَ حَتَّى أَخِرَهُ   I read the Qur'an until the end.
   قَدِمَ الْحُجَّاجُ حَتَّى الْمُشَاةُ   The pilgrims came, even those on foot.

إِمَّا (either...or):

  e.g.   اَلثَّمَرُ إِمَّا حُلْوٌ وَإِمَّا مُرٌّ   The fruit is either sweet or bitter.

أَوْ (or):

  e.g.   لَبِثْنَا يَوْمًا أَوْ بَعْضَ يَوْمٍ   We stayed for a day or a part of a day.

أَمْ (or): It is generally used with an interrogative (اِسْتِفْهَامٌ).

  e.g.   أَزَيْدٌ عِنْدَكَ أَمْ بَكْرٌ   Is Zayd with you or Bakr?

لَا (not): This negates from the مَعْطُوفٌ that which has been established for the مَعْطُوفٌ عَلَيْهِ.

  e.g.   جَاءَنِي زَيْدٌ لَا بَكْرٌ   Zayd came to me and not Bakr.

بَلْ (but, instead, rather): It is used for إِضْرَابٌ i.e. to give up one notion for another.

- If it appears after a positive sentence (إِيجَابٌ) or a command (أَمْرٌ), it negates the ruling for that which is before it, and affirms it for that which is after it.

  e.g.   جَاءَنِي زَيْدٌ بَلْ بَكْرٌ   Zayd came to me. Rather, Bakr (came).

- If it appears after a (نَفْيٌ) or a (نَهْيٌ), it confirms this ruling (of negation) for the one before it, and affirms its opposite (i.e. opposite of negation) for the one after it.

  e.g.   مَا قَرَأْتُ الْكِتَابَ كُلَّهُ بَلْ بَعْضَهُ   I did not read the whole book; rather, [I read] some of it.

لَكِنْ (but, however): It is generally used with a نَفْيٌ and serves the purpose of اِسْتِدْرَاكٌ i.e. to rectify.

  e.g.   مَا جَاءَنِي زَيْدٌ لَكِنْ بَكْرٌ جَاءَ   Zayd did not come to me but Bakr came.

Notes:

1. If the مَعْطُوفٌ عَلَيْهِ is a ضَمِيرٌ مَرْفُوعٌ مُتَّصِلٌ, then its ضَمِيرٌ مُنْفَصِلٌ has to be mentioned after it.

   e.g.   ضَرَبْتُ أَنَا وَزَيْدٌ   Zayd and I hit.

2. However, if after the ضَمِيرٌ مَرْفُوعٌ مُتَّصِلٌ, another word appears before the مَعْطُوفٌ, then the ضَمِيرٌ مُنْفَصِلٌ need not be brought.

   e.g.   ضَرَبْتُ الْيَوْمَ وَزَيْدٌ   Zayd and I hit, today.

       مَا أَشْرَكْنَا وَلَا آبَاؤُنَا   Neither us nor our forefathers associated partners.

3. If the مَعْطُوفٌ عَلَيْهِ is a ضَمِيرٌ preceded by a حَرْفُ جَرٍّ, then the مَعْطُوفٌ should also be preceded by the same حَرْفُ جَرٍّ.

   e.g.   مَرَرْتُ بِكَ وَبِزَيْدٍ   I passed by you and Zayd.

EXERCISE

1. Fill in a suitable حَرْفُ عَطْفٍ, translate, fill in the *i'raab* and analyze the following sentences.

    i. أتفاحا أكلت _____ عنبا؟

    ii. قدمت إليه الطعام _____ ما أكله

    iii. ما قابلته _____ قابلت وكيله

    iv. باع عقاره _____ منزله

    v. صلى الإمام _____ المأموم

    vi. أأنت فعلت هذا _____ زيد؟

Section 3.10.5
عَطْفُ الْبَيَانِ

Definition: It is that تَابِعٌ, which clarifies or specifies its مَتْبُوعٌ.

- Often, it is a more famous name of two names.

    Example: قَامَ أَبُو حَفْصٍ عُمَرُ   Abu Hafs 'Umar stood up.

    Example: جَاءَ زَيْدٌ أَبُو عَمْرٍو   Abu 'Amr Zayd came.

EXERCISE

1. Translate, fill in the *i'raab* and analyze the following sentences.

    i. قام علي زين العابدين

    ii. جعل الله الكعبة البيت الحرام قياما للناس

CHAPTER 4
اَلْعَوَامِلُ – Governing Words

Definition: An عَامِلٌ is a word that governs/causes *i'raab* changes in another word.

There are two types of عَوَامِلُ: 1) مَعْنَوِيٌّ 2) لَفْظِيٌّ

1. عَامِلٌ مَعْنَوِيٌّ: It is that عَامِلٌ, which is not in word form i.e. it is abstract.

    There are two types of عَامِلٌ مَعْنَوِيٌّ.

    i. اَلْاِبْتِدَاءُ: It means that being free of a عَامِلٌ لَفْظِيٌّ gives a مُبْتَدَأ رَفْعٌ.

    e.g. زَيْدٌ قَائِمٌ Zayd is standing.

    Here, زَيْدٌ is the مُبْتَدَأ, which is مَرْفُوعٌ because of اِبْتِدَاءُ. قَائِمٌ is the خَبَرٌ and it is also مَرْفُوعٌ because of اِبْتِدَاءُ.

    ii. In the case of فِعْلٌ مُضَارِعٌ, being free of a حَرْفُ نَصْبٍ or حَرْفُ جَزْمٍ gives a فِعْلٌ مُضَارِعٌ رَفْعٌ.

    e.g. يَعْمَلُ زَيْدٌ Zayd is working.

    Here يَعْمَلُ is مَرْفُوعٌ because it is free of any حَرْفُ نَصْبٍ or حَرْفُ جَزْمٍ.

2. عَامِلٌ لَفْظِيٌّ: It is that عَامِلٌ, which is in word form.

    There are three types of عَامِلٌ لَفْظِيٌّ.

    i. اَلْحُرُوفُ
    ii. اَلْأَفْعَالُ
    iii. اَلْأَسْمَاءُ

Section 4.1
اَلْحُرُوفُ الْعَامِلَةُ – Governing Particles

A. Particles, Which Govern Nouns

1. اَلْحُرُوفُ الْجَارَّةُ   refer to section 1.7
2. اَلْحُرُوفُ الْمُشَبَّهَةُ بِالْفِعْلِ   refer to section 1.8
3. مَا وَلَا اَلْمُشَبَّهَتَانِ بِ لَيْسَ   refer to section 3.7.3
4. وَاوُ الْمَعِيَّةِ   refer to section 3.8.4
5. حُرُوفُ الْإِسْتِثْنَاءِ   refer to section 3.8.8
6. حُرُوفُ النِّدَاءِ   refer to section 3.8.1
7. لَا الَّتِي لِنَفْيِ الْجِنْسِ   refer to section 3.7.4

B. Particles, Which Govern فِعْلٌ مُضَارِعٌ

1. اَلْحُرُوفُ النَّاصِبَةُ
2. اَلْحُرُوفُ الْجَازِمَةُ

Section 4.1.1[58]

اَلْحُرُوفُ النَّاصِبَةُ – Particles That Give *Nasb*

These are as follows: أَنْ   لَنْ   كَيْ   إِذَنْ

- These appear before فِعْلٌ مُضَارِعٌ and cause the following changes at the end:
  - They give the last letter a *fathah* if it is not a نُوْنٌ of تَثْنِيَةٌ or جَمْعٌ.
  - If the last letter is a نُوْنٌ of تَثْنِيَةٌ or جَمْعٌ, it is dropped. The exception is the نُوْنٌ of the two جَمْعٌ مُؤَنَّثٌ.

Table 4.1
اَلْحُرُوفُ النَّاصِبَةُ

حَرْفُ نَصْبٍ	Meaning		Example
أَنْ	that, to	أُرِيْدُ أَنْ أَدْخُلَ الْجَنَّةَ	I want to enter Paradise.
لَنْ	will not, never	لَنْ يَدْخُلَ الْكَافِرُ الْجَنَّةَ	The disbeliever will never enter Paradise.
كَيْ	so that	جِئْتُ كَيْ أَسْتَرِيْحَ	I came so I could rest.
إِذَنْ	then, in that case	إِذَنْ تَفُوْزَ فِي عَمَلِكَ	In that case, you will be successful in your work. [This is said in response to the one who may have said: أَجْتَهِدُ (I will work hard).]

Notes:

1. Sometimes أَنْ, together with its فِعْل, gives the meaning of a *masdar*. In this case, أَنْ is called أَنْ الْمَصْدَرِيَّةُ.

   e.g. صَوْمُكُمْ خَيْرٌ لَكُمْ i.e. أَنْ تَصُوْمُوْا خَيْرٌ لَكُمْ
   Your fasting is better for you.

2. أَنْ is hidden after the following six حُرُوْفٌ and gives the last letter of فِعْلٌ مُضَارِعٌ a نَصْبٌ.[59]

   a. After حَتَّى:

      e.g. سِرْتُ حَتَّى أَدْخُلَ الْبَلَدَ   (حَتَّى أَنْ أَدْخُلَ)
      I travelled until I entered the city.

   b. After لَامُ النَّفْيِ or لَامُ الْجُحُوْدِ: i.e. that لَامٌ, which appears after كَانَ الْمَنْفِيَّةُ.

---

[58] For more examples and exercises, please refer to *al-Nahw al-Wadih, Ibtida'iyyah*, vol. 1, 47-52.
[59] For more examples and exercises, please refer to *al-Nahw al-Wadih, Ibtida'iyyah*, vol. 2, 52-62.

e.g. (لِأَنْ يُعَذِّبَهُمْ)   مَا كَانَ اللهُ لِيُعَذِّبَهُمْ

Allah was not going to punish them.

c. After أَوْ, which has the meaning of إِلَى (until) or إِلَّا أَنْ (but that/unless).

e.g. (إِلَى أَنْ تُعْطِيَنِي)   لَأَلْزَمَنَّكَ أَوْ تُعْطِيَنِي حَقِّي

I will not leave you until you give me my right.

(إِلَّا أَنْ يَعْتَذِرَ)   يُعَاقَبُ الْمُسِيءُ أَوْ يَعْتَذِرَ

The sinner will be punished unless he provides an excuse.

d. After وَاوُ الصَّرْفِ: i.e., that وَاوْ which "turns away" from the word after it the effect, which the عَامِل had on the word before it (before the وَاوْ).

e.g. (وَأَنْ تَكْذِبَ)   لَا تَأْمُرْ بِالصِّدْقِ وَتَكْذِبَ

Do not command the truth while you lie.

(Here, the وَاوْ turned away/stopped the effect of لَا from تَكْذِبَ.)

- This وَاوْ is also known as وَاوُ الْمُصَاحَبَةِ or وَاوُ الْمَعِيَّةِ.
- The sentence must start with a نَفْيٌ or نَهْيٌ.

e. After لَامُ التَّعْلِيلِ: i.e., that لَامْ which has the meaning of كَيْ (it is also called لَامُ كَيْ).

e.g. (لِأَنْ أَسْتَرِيحَ)   جِئْتُ لِأَسْتَرِيحَ

I came so I could rest.

f. After الْفَاءُ السَّبَبِيَّةُ/الْجَوَابِيَّةُ: i.e., that ف, which comes in the جَزَاءٌ to any of the following six.

1. الْأَمْرُ   e.g. (فَأَنْ أُكْرِمَكَ)   زُرْنِي فَأُكْرِمَكَ

Visit me so that I treat you hospitably.

2. النَّهْيُ   e.g. لَا تَطْغَوْا فِيهِ فَيَحِلَّ عَلَيْكُمْ غَضَبِي

Do not cross the limit regarding it, lest My wrath descends upon you.

3. النَّفْيُ   e.g. مَا تَزُورُنَا فَنُكْرِمَكَ

You do not visit us, otherwise we would have treated you hospitably.

4. الِاسْتِفْهَامُ   e.g. أَيْنَ بَيْتُكَ فَأَزُورَكَ

Where is your house, so I can visit you.

5. اَلتَّمَنِّي   e.g.   لَيْتَ لِي مَالًا فَأُنْفِقَهُ

I wish I had wealth, so I would have spent it.

6. اَلْعَرْضُ   e.g.   أَلَا تَنْزِلُ بِنَا فَتُصِيبَ خَيْرًا

Why don't you visit us so that you receive good!

3. أَنْ has to be written after a لَامُ التَّعْلِيلِ if the لَامُ التَّعْلِيلِ is joined to a لَاءٌ نَافِيَةٌ.

   e.g.   لِئَلَّا يَعْلَمَ   (لِأَنْ لَا)   So that he does not know.

4. أَنْ which appears after a verb with the root letters ع – ل – م is not a حَرْفُ نَصْبٍ. Therefore, it does not give a فِعْلٌ مُضَارِعٌ a *fathah*. Such an أَنْ is known as أَنْ الْمُخَفَّفَةُ مِنَ الْمُثَقَّلَةِ i.e., that أَنْ which was أَنَّ.

   e.g.   عَلِمْتُ أَنْ سَيَقُومُ   I knew that he will stand up.

   e.g.   عَلِمَ أَنْ سَيَكُونُ مِنْكُمْ مَرْضَى   He knew that some of you will be sick.

EXERCISE

1. Translate, fill in the *i'raab* and point out the حَرْفُ نَصْبٍ and its effect in the following sentences.

   i.   يجتهد الطالب لينجح

   ii.   لن يفوز الكسلان

   iii.   جئت كي أتعلم

   iv.   لم يكن الشرطي ليسرق

   v.   لا تأكل حتى تجوع

   vi.   إن الله يأمركم أن تذبحوا بقرة

   vii.   اصنع المعروف فتنال الشكر

   viii.   فأراد ربك أن يبلغا أشدهما ويستخرجا كنزهما

Section 4.1.2[60]
اَلْحُرُوْفُ الْجَازِمَةُ – Particles That Give *Jazm*

These are as follows: لَاءُ النَّهْيِ   لَامُ الْأَمْرِ   لَمَّا   لَمْ   إِنْ

- These appear before فِعْلٌ مُضَارِعٌ and cause the following changes at the end:
  - They give the last letter a *sukoon* if it is not a نُوْنٌ of تَثْنِيَةٌ or جَمْعٌ.
  - If the last letter is a نُوْنٌ of تَثْنِيَةٌ or جَمْعٌ, it will be dropped. The exception is the نُوْنٌ of the two جَمْعُ مُؤَنَّثٌ.

Table 4.2
اَلْحُرُوْفُ الْجَازِمَةُ

حَرْفُ جَزْم	Meaning	Example	
إِنْ	if	إِنْ تَجْلِسْ أَجْلِسْ	If you sit, I will sit.
لَمْ	did not	لَمْ يَضْرِبْنِيْ	He did not hit me.
لَمَّا	not yet	ذَهَبَ الْوَلَدُ وَ لَمَّا يَعُدْ	The boy went but has not returned yet.
لِ	should, shall, let	لِيَجْلِسْ	He should sit.
لَا	do not	لَا تَجْلِسْ	Do not sit.

Notes:

1. إِنْ appears before two verbal sentences. The first one is called شَرْطٌ (condition) and the second جَزَاءٌ (answer/result).

2. If إِنْ appears before إِلَّا, it should be translated negatively.

    e.g.   إِنْ هٰذَا إِلَّا مَلَكٌ كَرِيْمٌ   He is <u>not</u> but an honorable angel.

    Note: This negation could also be expressed as "He is only an honorable angel."

3. لَمْ can also be used to give the meaning of لَمَّا. For this, بَعْدُ or إِلَى الآنَ is added after the فِعْلٌ مُضَارِعٌ which was given جَزْمٌ by لَمْ.

    e.g.   لَمْ يَذْهَبْ بَعْدُ   He has not gone yet.

4. فَ should be brought before the جَزَاءٌ of a شَرْطٌ when the جَزَاءٌ is one of the following:

    a. جُمْلَةٌ اِسْمِيَّةٌ   e.g.   إِنْ تَأْتِنِيْ فَأَنْتَ مُكْرَمٌ

    If you come to me you will be treated hospitably.

---

[60] For more examples and exercises, please refer to *al-Nahw al-Wadih, Ibtida'iyyah*, vol. 1, 52-57 & vol. 2, 63-66.

b. أَمْرٌ e.g. إِنْ رَأَيْتَ زَيْدًا فَأَكْرِمْهُ

If you see Zayd, treat him hospitably.

c. نَهْيٌ e.g. إِنْ أَتَاكَ زَيْدٌ فَلَا تُهِنْهُ

If Zayd comes to you, do not humiliate him.

d. دُعَاءٌ e.g. إِنْ أَكْرَمْتَنِي فَجَزَاكَ اللهُ خَيْرًا

If you treat me hospitably, then, may Allah reward you well.

5. اَلْفِعْلُ الْمَاضِيْ will be translated in the future tense when it is…

    a. used as a دُعَاءٌ e.g. جَزَاكَ اللهُ خَيْرًا

May Allah reward you well.

    b. preceded by حَرْفُ شَرْطٍ e.g. إِنْ جَلَسْتَ جَلَسْتُ

If you sit, I will sit.

    c. preceded by اِسْمٌ مَوْصُوْلٌ e.g. مَنْ جَاءَ بِالْحَسَنَةِ فَلَهُ عَشْرُ أَمْثَالِهَا

Whoever comes with good, there will be ten like it for him.

EXERCISE

1. Translate, fill in the *i'raab* and point out the حَرْفُ جَزْمٍ and its effect on the following sentences.

    i. ليفتح علي النافذة   iv. كبر الغلام ولما يتهذب

    ii. لا تكثر من الضحك   v. إن يسافر أخوك أسافر معه

    iii. اختلف الشريكان ولم يتفقا   vi. إن تنصروا الله ينصركم

Section 4.2
اَلْأَفْعَالُ الْعَامِلَةُ – Governing Verbs

Section 4.2.1
اَلْفِعْلُ الْمَعْرُوفُ – **Active Verb:** It is that verb whose doer is known/mentioned.

- فِعْلٌ مَعْرُوفٌ, whether transitive or intransitive, governs the following nouns, as and when applicable:
    - it gives رَفْعٌ to the فَاعِلٌ.
    - it gives نَصْبٌ to the following, as and when applicable:
        i. مَفْعُولٌ بِهِ (اَلْفِعْلُ الْمُتَعَدِّيْ) can only be governed by a
        ii. مَفْعُولٌ مُطْلَقٌ
        iii. مَفْعُولٌ مَعَهُ
        iv. مَفْعُولٌ لَهُ
        v. مَفْعُولٌ فِيْهِ
        vi. حَالٌ
        vii. تَمْيِيزٌ

Section 4.2.2
اَلْفِعْلُ الْمَجْهُولُ – **Passive Verb:** It is that verb whose doer is not known/mentioned.

- فِعْلٌ مَجْهُولٌ is also known as فِعْلُ مَا لَمْ يُسَمَّ فَاعِلُهُ (a verb whose فَاعِلٌ is not named).
- It gives رَفْعٌ to the نَائِبُ فَاعِلٍ (originally the مَفْعُولٌ بِهِ).
- It gives نَصْبٌ to all the remaining مَنْصُوبَاتٌ.
    e.g. ضُرِبَ زَيْدٌ يَوْمَ الْجُمُعَةِ أَمَامَ الْقَاضِيْ ضَرْبًا شَدِيْدًا فِيْ دَارِهِ تَأْدِيْبًا
    Zayd was beaten severely on Friday, in front of the Judge, in his office/house, to teach him manners.

Section 4.2.3
اَلْفِعْلُ اللَّازِمُ – **Intransitive Verb:** It is that verb whose meaning can be understood without a مَفْعُولٌ بِهِ.
    e.g. جَلَسَ زَيْدٌ   Zayd sat.

Section 4.2.4
اَلْأَفْعَالُ النَّاقِصَةُ: These were discussed earlier in section 1.9.

Section 4.2.5[61]
اَلْفِعْلُ الْمُتَعَدِّيْ – Transitive Verb

Definition: It is that verb whose meaning cannot be understood without a مَفْعُوْلٌ بِهِ.

    e.g.   ضَرَبَ زَيْدٌ بَكْرًا   Zayd hit Bakr.

There are four types of اَلْفِعْلُ الْمُتَعَدِّيْ. These are as follows:

1. Those verbs, which require one مَفْعُوْلٌ بِهِ as is the case with most *muta'addi* verbs.

    e.g.   ضَرَبَ زَيْدٌ بَكْرًا

2. Those verbs, which **can** be given two مَفْعُوْلٌ بِهِ. These include the following:
   - Any verb, which has the meaning of إِعْطَاءٌ (to give).

       e.g.   وَهَبَ   مَنَحَ   أَعْطَى   etc.

       أَعْطَيْتُ السَّائِلَ خُبْزًا I gave the beggar a bread.

   - Some other verbs, which can also have two مَفْعُوْلٌ بِهِ include the following

       سَأَلَ   كَسَى   أَمَرَ   etc.

       e.g.   يَكْسُو الْعِلْمُ أَهْلَهُ وَقَارًا   Knowledge clothes its possessor with dignity.

3. Those verbs, which **must** be given two اَلْمَفْعُوْلُ بِهِ.
   - These verbs are known as أَفْعَالُ الْقُلُوْبِ (verbs which relate to the heart/feelings).
   - They enter upon a مُبْتَدَأٌ and خَبَرٌ unlike the verbs above (number 2).

Table 4.3
أَفْعَالُ الْقُلُوْبِ

Verb	Usage	Example	
رَأَى	used for certainty (يَقِيْنٌ)	رَأَيْتُ سَعِيْدًا ذَاهِبًا	I was sure Sa'eed was going.
وَجَدَ	used for certainty (يَقِيْنٌ)	وَجَدْتُ رَشِيْدًا عَالِمًا	I was sure Rasheed was knowledgeable.
عَلِمَ	used for certainty (يَقِيْنٌ)	عَلِمْتُ زَيْدًا أَمِيْنًا	I was sure Zayd was trustworthy.
زَعَمَ	used for certainty (يَقِيْنٌ) or doubt (شَكٌّ)	زَعَمْتُ زَيْدًا حَاضِرًا	I was sure Zayd was present. / I thought Zayd was present.
حَسِبَ	used for doubt (شَكٌّ)	حَسِبْتُ زَيْدًا فَاضِلًا	I thought Zayd was well-educated.
خَالَ	used for doubt (شَكٌّ)	خِلْتُ خَالِدًا قَائِمًا	I thought Khalid was standing.
ظَنَّ	used for doubt (شَكٌّ)	ظَنَنْتُ بَكْرًا نَائِمًا	I thought Bakr was sleeping.

---

[61] For more details, examples, and exercises, please refer to *al-Nahw al-Wadih, Ibtida'iyyah*, vol. 3, 69-71.

Note: Other verbs, which also require two مَفْعُولٌ بِهِ include the following:

صَيَّرَ   to make something something else

     e.g. صَيَّرْتُ الْأَوْرَاقَ كِتَابًا I made the pages a book.

اتَّخَذَ   to take someone/something as someone/something

     e.g. وَاتَّخَذَ اللهُ إِبْرَاهِيمَ خَلِيلًا   Allah took Ibraheem (peace be upon him) as a friend.

جَعَلَ   to make something something else

     e.g. جَعَلْتُ الْكِتَابَ مُرَتَّبًا   I made the book organized.

4. Those verbs which require three مَفْعُولٌ بِهِ. Each of these has the meaning of "informing" or "showing." These are as follows:

Table 4.4

Verb	Example	
أَرَى	أَرَيْتُ زَيْدًا خَالِدًا نَائِمًا	I informed Zayd that Khalid is sleeping.
أَعْلَمَ	أَعْلَمْتُ زَيْدًا بَكْرًا فَاضِلًا	I informed Zayd that Bakr is well-educated.
أَنْبَأَ	أَنْبَأَنِي الرَّسُولُ الْأَمِيرَ قَادِمًا	The messenger informed me that the chief is coming.
نَبَّأَ	نَبَّأْتُهُمُ الْكِبْرَ مَمْقُوتًا	I informed them that arrogance is hated.
أَخْبَرَ	أَخْبَرْتُ الْغُلْمَانَ اللَّعْبَ مُفِيدًا	I informed the boys that sport is beneficial.
خَبَّرَ	خَبَّرْتُ الْمُسَافِرِينَ الْقِطَارَ مُتَأَخِّرًا	I informed the travellers that the train is late.
حَدَّثَ	حَدَّثْتُ الْأَوْلَادَ السِّبَاحَةَ نَافِعَةً	I informed the children that swimming is beneficial.

EXERCISE

1. Translate, fill in the *i'raab* and analyze the following sentences.

     i. نبأت سعيدا أخاه قادما   iv. رأيت الصلح خيرا

     ii. أعطيت زيدا درهما   v. أخبرني زيد أباه مريضا

     iii. فهم سعيد الدرس   vi. ظننت الجو معتدلا

Section 4.2.6

أَفْعَالُ الْمُقَارَبَةِ وَالرَّجَاءِ وَالشُّرُوعِ

Definition: These verbs are actually a type of أَفْعَالٌ نَاقِصَةٌ and they behave the same way. They also enter upon مُبْتَدَأٌ and خَبَرٌ, and give رَفْعٌ to their اِسْمٌ and نَصْبٌ to their خَبَرٌ. The difference is that their خَبَرٌ is always جُمْلَةٌ فِعْلِيَّةٌ.

They are used for the following purposes:

1. أَفْعَالُ الْمُقَارَبَةِ show nearness in the attainment (حُصُولٌ) of the خَبَرٌ.
2. أَفْعَالُ الرَّجَاءِ show desire for attainment of خَبَرٌ.
3. أَفْعَالُ الشُّرُوعِ show commencement of action.

Table 4.5
أَفْعَالُ الْمُقَارَبَةِ وَالرَّجَاءِ وَالشُّرُوعِ

فِعْلٌ	اِسْمٌ	خَبَرٌ	Type	Example	
كَادَ	مَرْفُوعٌ	مُضَارِعٌ preferably without أَنْ	حُصُولٌ	كَادَ زَيْدٌ يَذْهَبُ	Zayd was about to go.
كَرَبَ / كَرُبَ*	مَرْفُوعٌ	مُضَارِعٌ preferably without أَنْ	حُصُولٌ	كَرَبَ خَالِدٌ يَجْلِسُ	Khalid was about to sit.
أَوْشَكَ	مَرْفُوعٌ	مُضَارِعٌ preferably with أَنْ	حُصُولٌ	أَوْشَكَ زَيْدٌ أَنْ يَجْلِسَ	Zayd was about to sit.
عَسَى*	مَرْفُوعٌ	مُضَارِعٌ preferably with أَنْ	رَجَاءٌ	عَسَى زَيْدٌ أَنْ يَخْرُجَ	Hopefully Zayd will come out.
طَفِقَ*	مَرْفُوعٌ	مُضَارِعٌ without أَنْ	شُرُوعٌ	طَفِقَ زَيْدٌ يَكْتُبُ	Zayd began writing.
جَعَلَ*	مَرْفُوعٌ	مُضَارِعٌ without أَنْ	شُرُوعٌ	جَعَلَ زَيْدٌ يَقْرَأُ	Zayd began reading.
أَخَذَ*	مَرْفُوعٌ	مُضَارِعٌ without أَنْ	شُرُوعٌ	أَخَذَ زَيْدٌ يَأْكُلُ	Zayd began eating.

* These verbs are used only in past tense.

- The أَفْعَالُ الشُّرُوعِ can be used as normal verbs too.

  e.g. أَخَذَ زَيْدٌ ثَوْبَهُ   Zayd took his clothes.

---

[62] For more details, examples and exercises, please refer to *al-Nahw al-Wadih*, Thanawiyyah, vol. 1, 103-108.

Sentence Analysis: عَسَى زَيْدٌ أَنْ يَخْرُجَ   Hopefully Zayd will come out.

$$\underbrace{\text{أَنْ يَخْرُجَ}}_{\text{فِعْلٌ + فَاعِلٌ (هُوَ)}} \quad \text{زَيْدٌ} \quad \text{عَسَى}$$

خَبَرُ عَسَى   اِسْمُ عَسَى   فِعْلُ الرَّجَاءِ

EXERCISE

1. Translate, fill in the *i'raab* and analyze the following sentences.

   i. عسى الله أن يشفيك   iv. أوشك أن يفتح باب المدرسة

   ii. تكاد السموات يتفطرن   v. أخذت أكتب

   iii. عست المرأة أن تقوم   vi. جعل زيد يمسح رأسه

Section 4.2.7 - أَفْعَالُ الْمَدْحِ وَالذَّمِّ – Verbs of Praise and Blame

Verbs of praise:	نِعْمَ	e.g.	نِعْمَ الرَّجُلُ زَيْدٌ	What a wonderful man Zayd is!
	حَبَّذَا	e.g.	حَبَّذَا زَيْدٌ	What a wonderful man Zayd is!
Verbs of blame:	بِئْسَ	e.g.	بِئْسَ الرَّجُلُ زَيْدٌ	What an evil man Zayd is!
	سَاءَ	e.g.	سَاءَ الرَّجُلُ زَيْدٌ	What an evil man Zayd is!

- That which appears after the فَاعِلٌ is called مَخْصُوصٌ بِالْمَدْحِ or مَخْصُوصٌ بِالذَّمِّ.
- The فَاعِلٌ of نِعْمَ – بِئْسَ – سَاءَ must be one of the following:
   i. prefixed with ال.
      e.g. نِعْمَ الرَّجُلُ زَيْدٌ   What a wonderful man Zayd is!
   ii. مُضَافٌ to a noun prefixed with ال.
      e.g. نِعْمَ صَاحِبُ الْعِلْمِ زَيْدٌ   What a wonderful learned man Zayd is!
   iii. a hidden ضَمِيرٌ followed by a نَكِرَةٌ مَنْصُوبَةٌ (being تَمْيِيزٌ).
      e.g. [نِعْمَ (هُوَ) رَجُلًا زَيْدٌ]   نِعْمَ رَجُلًا زَيْدٌ   What a wonderful man Zayd is!
   iv. The word مَا.
      e.g. بِئْسَ مَا كَانُوا يَفْعَلُونَ   How evil is what they used to do!

In حَبَّذَا زَيْدٌ, حَبَّ is the فِعْلٌ.
ذَا (اِسْمُ إِشَارَةٍ) is its فَاعِلٌ.
زَيْدٌ is the مَخْصُوصٌ بِالْمَدْحِ.

Notes:
1. These verbs are used in the past tense in their singular form (masculine or feminine).
2. At times the مَخْصُوصٌ بِالْمَدْحِ is dropped.
   e.g. نِعْمَ الْعَبْدُ   i.e. نِعْمَ الْعَبْدُ أَيُّوبُ   What a wonderful slave Ayyub is!

---

[63] For more details, examples and exercises, please refer to *al-Nahw al-Wadih, Thanawiyyah*, vol. 1, 57-59.

Sentence Analysis:

$$\underset{\underset{\text{خَبَرٌ مُقَدَّمٌ}}{\underbrace{\text{فِعْلُ الْمَدْحِ} \quad + \quad \text{فَاعِلٌ}}}}{\text{نِعْمَ} \quad \quad \text{الرَّجُلُ}} \quad + \quad \underset{\text{مُبْتَدَأٌ مُؤَخَّرٌ}}{\text{زَيْدٌ}} \quad - \quad \text{جُمْلَةٌ اسْمِيَّةٌ خَبَرِيَّةٌ}$$

مَخْصُوصٌ بِالْمَدْحِ

EXERCISE

1. Translate, fill in the *i'raab* and analyze the following sentences.

   i. نعمت الابنة فاطمة

   ii. حبذا الاتفاق

   iii. نعم المولى

Section 4.2.8[64]
أَفْعَالُ التَّعَجُّبِ – Verbs of Wonder

For three-letter verbs (اَلثُّلَاثِيُّ الْمُجَرَّدُ), there are two *wazns* for expressing wonder or amazement.

1. مَا أَفْعَلَهُ: مَا has the meaning of أَيُّ شَيْءٍ.

    e.g.   مَا أَحْسَنَ زَيْدًا   How wonderful Zayd is!

2. أَفْعِلْ بِهِ: أَفْعِلْ (فِعْلُ أَمْرٍ) has the meaning of past tense and the ب is extra (زَائِدَةٌ).

    e.g.   (أَحْسَنَ زَيْدٌ)   أَحْسِنْ بِزَيْدٍ   How wonderful Zayd is!
    جُمْلَةٌ فِعْلِيَّةٌ إِنْشَائِيَّةٌ

- To express wonder for other than three-letter verbs (غَيْرُ الثُّلَاثِيِّ الْمُجَرَّدِ), a word such as أَشِدْ بِ/ مَا أَشَدَّ or أَحْسِنْ بِ/مَا أَحْسَنَ etc. should be placed before the مَصْدَر of the desired verb. The مَصْدَر will be مَفْعُولٌ بِهِ, thus مَنْصُوبٌ.

    e.g.   مَا أَشَدَّ إِكْرَامَ النَّاسِ لِلْعُلَمَاءِ   How very respectful people are towards the learned!

EXERCISE

1. Translate, fill in the *i'raab* and analyze the following sentences.

    i. أطول بزيد

    ii. ما أشد بياض شعره

    iii. ما أطول الرجلين

---

[64] For more details, examples and exercises, please refer to *al-Nahw al-Wadih*, Thanawiyyah, vol. 1, 60-63.

Section 4.3
اَلْأَسْمَاءُ الْعَامِلَةُ – Governing Nouns

Amongst these, أَسْمَاءُ الْأَفْعَالِ were discussed in section 2.4.4. Here, we will discuss the rest.

Section 4.3.1[65]
اَلْأَسْمَاءُ الشَّرْطِيَّةُ – Conditional Nouns

- They govern two فِعْلٌ مُضَارِعٌ giving both a جَزْمٌ.
- They appear before two sentences. The first is called شَرْطٌ (condition) and the second جَزَاءٌ (result).

Table 4.6
اَلْأَسْمَاءُ الشَّرْطِيَّةُ

Noun	Meaning	Usage	Example	
1. مَنْ	who, whoever	لِلْعَاقِلِ	مَنْ يُكْرِمْنِي أُكْرِمْهُ	Whoever treats me hospitably, I will treat him hospitably.
2. مَا	what, whatever	لِغَيْرِ الْعَاقِلِ	مَا تَأْكُلْ أَكُلْ	Whatever you eat, I will eat.
3. مَهْمَا	however much	لِغَيْرِ الْعَاقِلِ	مَهْمَا تُنْفِقْ فِي الْخَيْرِ يَنْفَعْكَ	Whatever you spend in the way of good, will benefit you.
4. مَتَى	when	لِلزَّمَانِ	مَتَى تَذْهَبْ أَذْهَبْ	Whenever you go, I will go.
5. أَيَّانَ	when	لِلزَّمَانِ	أَيَّانَ تُسَافِرْ أُسَافِرْ	Whenever you travel, I will travel.
6. أَيْنَ	where	لِلْمَكَانِ	أَيْنَ تَذْهَبْ أَذْهَبْ	Wherever you go, I will go.
7. أَنَّى	where	لِلْمَكَانِ	أَنَّى تَنْزِلْ أَنْزِلْ	Wherever you stay, I will stay.
8. حَيْثُمَا	where	لِلْمَكَانِ	حَيْثُمَا تُسَافِرْ أُسَافِرْ	Wherever you travel, I will travel.
9. كَيْفَمَا	how, manner	لِلْحَالِ	كَيْفَمَا تَقْعُدْ أَقْعُدْ	Whichever way you sit, I will sit.
10. أَيٌّ	any of the above	any of the above	أَيُّ مَكَانٍ تَذْهَبْ أَذْهَبْ	Whichever place you go, I will go.

Notes:

1. إِنْ and إِذَمَا have the same function as اَلْأَسْمَاءُ الشَّرْطِيَّةُ i.e. giving *jazm* to two فِعْلٌ مُضَارِعٌ except that they are particles (حَرْفَا الشَّرْطِ) and not nouns. Collectively they (nouns and particles) are all called أَدَوَاتُ الشَّرْطِ الْجَازِمَةُ.

---

[65] For more examples and exercises, please refer to *al-Nahw al-Wadih, Ibtida'iyyah*, vol. 2, 66-71.

إِنْ	if	e.g.	إِنْ تَذْهَبْ أَذْهَبْ	If you go, I will go.
إِذْمَا	if	e.g.	إِذْمَا تَفْعَلْ شَرًّا تَنْدَمْ	If you do evil, you will be regretful.

2. There are other أَدَوَاتُ الشَّرْطِ that are غَيْرُ جَازِمَةٍ, i.e. they do not give جَزْمٌ to فِعْلٌ مُضَارِعٌ. Some of these are discussed in Section 4.4, # 13 (حُرُوْفُ الشَّرْطِ الَّتِيْ لَا تَجْزِمُ). Amongst the اَلْأَسْمَاءُ الشَّرْطِيَّةُ, which do not give , two are discussed below:

    i. كُلَّمَا (whenever, every time)

        This is a ظَرْفٌ, and enters upon فِعْلٌ مَاضٍ. It also conveys the meaning of emphasis and repetition.

        e.g.   كُلَّمَا مَرِضْتُ ذَهَبْتُ إِلَى الطَّبِيْبِ   Whenever I fell sick, I went to the doctor.

    ii. إِذَا (when)

        This is also a ظَرْفٌ, and is used to give the meaning of فِعْلٌ مُضَارِعٌ. It also entails the meaning of condition (مُتَضَمِّنٌ مَعْنَى الشَّرْطِ).

        e.g.   إِذَا لَقِيْتَهُ فَسَلِّمْ عَلَيْهِ   When you meet him, greet him.

3. When the following nouns are used for اِسْتِفْهَامٌ (interrogative), they appear before one sentence.

    أَيٌّ   أَنَّى   أَيْنَ   أَيَّانَ   مَتَى   مَا   مَنْ

    e.g.   مَتَى تُسَافِرُ   أَيْنَ تَذْهَبُ   مَنْ أَنْتَ   مَا هَذَا

EXERCISE

1. Complete the following sentences with a suitable جَزَاءٌ.

i.	_____ من يصنع معروفا	v.	_____ أنى ينزل ذو العلم
ii.	_____ ما تخف من أعمالك	vi.	_____ متى تسافر
iii.	_____ كيفما تعامل إخوانك	vii.	_____ من احترم الناس
iv.	_____ أيان يكثر فراغ الشباب	viii.	_____ من يكثر كلامه

Section 4.3.2[66]
اِسْمُ الْفَاعِلِ – Active Participle

Definition: It is a noun which indicates the one doing or undertaking an action described by the root letters. This is irrespective of its position in a sentence.

- It is created from ثُلَاثِيٌّ مُجَرَّدٌ verbs on the pattern of فَاعِلٌ. For other than ثُلَاثِيٌّ مُجَرَّدٌ verbs, it is created on the pattern of its مُضَارِعٌ by changing the حَرْفُ مُضَارِع into a *meem* with a *dammah*, and giving a *kasrah* to the letter before the last.

Effect:

- It has the same effect as that of its active verb (فِعْلٌ مَعْرُوفٌ) i.e. if its verb is لَازِمٌ, it gives رَفْعٌ to the فَاعِلٌ; and if it is مُتَعَدٍّ, it gives رَفْعٌ to the فَاعِلٌ and نَصْبٌ to the مَفْعُولٌ بِهِ.
- اِسْمُ الْفَاعِلِ acts only in either of the following two situations:
    1. When it is prefixed with ال.

       e.g. أَنَا الشَّاكِرُ نِعْمَتَكَ   I am grateful for your favor.
    2. When it indicates present or future tense and is preceded by مُبْتَدَأٌ or مَوْصُوفٌ or اِسْتِفْهَامٌ or نَفْيٌ. For example,

       a. مُبْتَدَأٌ   e.g.   زَيْدٌ ضَارِبٌ أَبُوهُ بَكْرًا   Zayd's father is beating/will beat Bakr.

       b. مَوْصُوفٌ   e.g.   مَرَرْتُ بِرَجُلٍ ضَارِبٍ أَبُوهُ بَكْرًا   I passed by a man whose father is beating/will beat Bakr.

       c. اِسْتِفْهَامٌ   e.g.   أَضَارِبٌ زَيْدٌ بَكْرًا؟   Is Zayd beating Bakr?/Will Zayd beat Bakr?

       d. نَفْيٌ   e.g.   مَا قَائِمٌ زَيْدٌ   Zayd is not standing/will not stand.

Sentence Analysis:

---

[66] This section and the following sub-section are based on the discussion in *al-Nahw al-Wadih*. See *al-Nahw al-Wadih, Thanawiyyah*, vol. 2, 71-76.

Section 4.3.2.1
اِسْمُ الْمُبَالَغَةِ

Definition: It is that noun, which conveys extremity/intensity in meaning.

- اِسْمُ الْفَاعِلِ is turned into the *seeghahs* of مُبَالَغَة when exaggeration in meaning is intended.
- Some of the *wazns* of مُبَالَغَة are as follows:

Table 4.7
أَوْزَانُ اِسْمِ الْمُبَالَغَةِ

Wazns	Examples	
	Arabic	Meaning
فَعِيْلٌ	عَلِيْمٌ	most learned
فَاعُوْلٌ	فَارُوْقٌ	great distinguisher
فَعَّالٌ	ضَحَّاكٌ	someone who laughs a lot
فَعُوْلٌ	صَبُوْرٌ	very patient
فَعُّوْلٌ	قَيُّوْمٌ	careful maintainer/sustainer
مِفْعِيْلٌ	مِنْطِيْقٌ	very eloquent
مِفْعَالٌ	مِعْوَانٌ	someone who helps frequently

- اِسْمُ الْمُبَالَغَةِ does the عَمَلٌ of اِسْمُ الْفَاعِلِ with the same conditions.

    e.g. يُعْجِبُنِي الشَّكُوْرُ الْمُنْعِمَ

    The one who is very grateful to the one who does good (to him), pleases me.

    إِنَّ الْجَبَانَ لَهَيَّابٌ لِقَاءَ الْعَدُوِّ

    Indeed, the coward is very scared of meeting the enemy.

Notes:

1. The round ة at the end of some *wazns* is for مُبَالَغَة and not for gender.

    e.g. فَعَّالَةٌ   عَلَّامَةٌ   well-learned

2. The *wazn* فَعَّالٌ is also used to denote a profession.

    e.g. طَبَّاخٌ   cook   نَجَّارٌ   carpenter

    حَدَّادٌ   blacksmith   حَلَّاقٌ   barber

EXERCISES

1. Translate, fill in the *i'raab* and point out the effect and tense of the اِسْمُ الْفَاعِلِ in the following sentences.

   i.   أذاهب صديقنا؟
   ii. الضارب زيد بكرا
   iii. لست بجاحد فضلكم
   iv. أمنجز أنتم وعدكم؟
   v.   ما شارب زيد القهوة
   vi. زيد شارب القهوة
   vii. المؤمن محسن عمله
   viii. الطالب قارئ كتابا

Section 4.3.3
اِسْمُ الْمَفْعُوْلِ – Passive Participle

Definition: It is that noun which indicates the one upon whom an action described by the root letters is done. This is irrespective of its position in a sentence.

- It is created from ثُلَاثِيٌّ مُجَرَّدٌ verbs on the pattern of مَفْعُوْلٌ. For other than ثُلَاثِيٌّ مُجَرَّدٌ, it is created on the pattern of its مُضَارِعٌ by changing the حَرْفُ مُضَارِعٍ into a *meem* with a *dammah*, and giving a *fathah* to the letter before the last.

Effect:

- It has the same effect as that of its passive verb فِعْلٌ مَجْهُوْلٌ, i.e. it gives رَفْعٌ to the نَائِبُ الْفَاعِلِ.
- The rules mentioned above regarding the اِسْمُ الْفَاعِلِ also apply here.

Examples:

i. prefixed with *alif-laam*	e.g.	الْمُسَمَّى هِشَامًا أَخِيْ	The one named Hisham is my brother.
ii. مُبْتَدَأٌ	e.g.	زَيْدٌ مَضْرُوْبٌ اِبْنُهُ	Zayd's son is being beaten/will be beaten.
iii. مَوْصُوْفٌ	e.g.	مَرَرْتُ بِرَجُلٍ مَضْرُوْبٍ اِبْنُهُ	I passed by a man whose son is being beaten/will be beaten.
iv. اِسْتِفْهَامٌ	e.g.	أَمَضْرُوْبٌ زَيْدٌ؟	Is Zayd being beaten?/Will Zayd be beaten?
v. نَفْيٌ	e.g.	مَا مَضْرُوْبٌ زَيْدٌ	Zayd is not being beaten/will not be beaten.

EXERCISE

1. Translate, fill in the *i'raab* and point out the effect and tense of the اِسْمُ الْمَفْعُوْلِ in the following sentences.

    i. زيد مسموع خبره
    ii. خالد معلّم ابنه الحياكة
    iii. العلم معروفة فوائده
    iv. الفقير معطًى ثوبًا
    v. الكتاب متقن طبعه
    vi. الأشجار مقطوعة أغصانها

---

[67] This section is based on the discussion in *al-Nahw al-Wadih*. See *al-Nahw al-Wadih, Thanawiyyah*, vol 2, 77-82.

Section 4.3.4[68]
اِسْمُ الْفَاعِلِ That Adjective Which Is Similar to – اَلصِّفَةُ الْمُشَبَّهَةُ بِاسْمِ الْفَاعِلِ

Definition: It is that noun, which is created from the مَصْدَر of a اَلثُّلَاثِيُّ اللَّازِمُ (three-letter intransitive verb) to indicate permanent existence of the meaning in the doer.

- Like its فِعْلٌ لَازِمٌ, it generally gives the فَاعِلٌ a رَفْعٌ.
  e.g.   حَسَنٌ وَجْهُهُ   His face is beautiful.

- It conveys permanency of meaning in the object it relates to e.g. حَسَنٌ (beautiful) is a permanent quality, as compared to اِسْمُ الْفَاعِلِ, which indicates a temporary meaning e.g. ضَارِبٌ is a temporary quality, which exists only at the time of the action.

- All such nouns, which are derived from a اَلثُّلَاثِيُّ اللَّازِمُ (three-letter intransitive verb) and give the meaning of اِسْمُ الْفَاعِلِ but are not on the *wazn* of اِسْمُ الْفَاعِلِ, are صِفَةٌ مُشَبَّهَةٌ.

Some of the common *wazns* of صِفَةٌ مُشَبَّهَةٌ (based on usage) are given below

Table 4.8
أَوْزَانُ الصِّفَةِ الْمُشَبَّهَةِ

Wazns	Examples	
	Arabic	Meaning
فَعِلٌ	فَرِحٌ	happy
فَعَلٌ	حَسَنٌ	beautiful
فَعِيلٌ	شَرِيفٌ	noble/honorable
فَعَالٌ	جَبَانٌ	coward
فُعَالٌ	شُجَاعٌ	brave

- Colors and bodily defects appear on the following *wazns*:

  أَفْعَلُ (masculine)   e.g.   أَحْمَرُ   red
                                أَبْكَمُ   mute

  فَعْلَاءُ (feminine)   e.g.   حَمْرَاءُ   red
                                بَكْمَاءُ   mute

---

[68] For more details, examples, and exercises, please refer to *al-Nahw al-Wadih, Thanawiyyah*, vol. 2, 83-91.

- The صِفَةٌ مُشَبَّهَةٌ of non-three letter verbs (غَيْرُ الثُّلَاثِيِّ الْمُجَرَّدِ) is brought on the *wazn* of its اِسْمُ الْفَاعِلِ on the condition that permanency of meaning is intended.

    e.g.   مُسْتَقِيْمٌ   straight

EXERCISE

1. Translate, fill in the *i'raab*, and identify all the صِفَةٌ مُشَبَّهَةٌ in the following passage.

   كان هارون الرشيد فصيحاً كريماً، هُماماً ورعاً، يحج سنة ويغزو سنة وكان أديباً فطناً، حافظاً للقرآن، سليم الذوق، صحيح التمييز، جريئاً في الحق، مهيباً عند الخاصة والعامة، وكان طلق المحيا، يحب الشعراء ويعطيهم العطاء الجزيل ويدني منه أهل الأدب والدين، ويتواضع للعلماء.

2. Translate, fill in the *i'raab* and identify the *seeghahs* of مُبَالَغَةٌ and اِسْمُ الْفَاعِلِ.

   قال حكيم: المؤمن صبور شكور لا نمّام ولا حسُود ولا حقُود ولا مختال. يطلب من الخيرات أعلاها ومن الأخلاق أسناها. لا يرد سائلا ولا يبخل بمال، متواصل الهمم، مترادف الإحسان، وزّان لكلامه، خزّان للسانه، محسن عمله، مكثر في الحق أمله، ليس بهياب عند الفزع ولا وثاب عند الطمع، مواس للفقراء، رحيم بالضعفاء.

Section 4.3.5[69]
اِسْمُ التَّفْضِيْلِ – Comparative and Superlative Noun

Definition: It is that noun, which indicates that a quality described by the root letters is found to a greater extent in one person/thing when compared to another.

e.g. خَالِدٌ أَكْبَرُ مِنْ عَمْرٍو   Khalid is older/bigger than 'Amr.

It can also refer to the highest degree (superlative) of the quality described by the root letters.

e.g. اَللهُ أَكْبَرُ   Allah is the greatest.

<u>Note</u>: This is the case when it is used without مِنْ, i.e. without comparison.

Table 4.9
أَوْزَانُ اِسْمِ التَّفْضِيْلِ

	Masculine	Example	Feminine	Example	Meaning
Singular	أَفْعَلُ	أَكْبَرُ	فُعْلَى	كُبْرَى	Bigger/older
Dual	أَفْعَلَانِ	أَكْبَرَانِ	فُعْلَيَانِ	كُبْرَيَانِ	Bigger/older
Plural	أَفْعَلُوْنَ	أَكْبَرُوْنَ	فُعْلَيَاتٌ	كُبْرَيَاتٌ	Bigger/older
	أَفَاعِلُ	أَكَابِرُ	فُعَلٌ	كُبَرٌ	Bigger/older

Usage:

اِسْمُ التَّفْضِيْلِ is used in three ways.

1. **With مِنْ:** the اِسْمُ التَّفْضِيْلِ will always be a singular masculine (وَاحِدٌ مُذَكَّرٌ).

    e.g. زَيْدٌ أَعْلَمُ مِنْ بَكْرٍ   Zayd is more knowledgeable than Bakr.

    عَائِشَةُ أَكْبَرُ مِنْ زَيْنَبَ   'Aishah is older than Zaynab.

2. **With ال:** the اِسْمُ التَّفْضِيْلِ must correspond with the word before it in gender and number.

    e.g. اَلزَّيْدَانِ الْأَعْلَمَانِ غَائِبَانِ   The two more knowledgeable Zayds are absent.

    عَائِشَةُ الْكُبْرَى حَاضِرَةٌ   The older 'Aishah is present.

3. **With إِضَافَةٌ:** the اِسْمُ التَّفْضِيْلِ may be وَاحِدٌ مُذَكَّرٌ or it may correspond with the word before it.

    e.g. اَلزَّيْدُوْنَ أَعْلَمُ الْقَوْمِ
    The Zayds are the most knowledgeable of people.

    اَلزَّيْدَانِ أَعْلَمَا الْقَوْمِ
    The two Zayds are the most knowledgeable of people.

---

[69] For more details, examples, and exercises, please refer to *al-Nahw al-Wadih, Thanawiyyah*, vol. 2, 92-100.

عَائِشَةُ كُبْرَى النَّاسِ عَائِشَةُ أَكْبَرُ النَّاسِ

'Aishah is the oldest of people.

Notes:

1. اِسْمُ التَّفْضِيْلِ of words, which indicate color, physical defects and of غَيْرُ الثُّلَاثِيِّ الْمُجَرَّدِ verbs is made by placing the words أَشَدُّ, أَكْثَرُ, etc. before the مَصْدَرٌ of that word. The مَصْدَرٌ will be the تَمْيِيْزٌ, and therefore, will be مَنْصُوْبٌ.

   e.g. هُوَ أَشَدُّ حُمْرَةً مِنْ زَيْدٍ   He is redder than Zayd.

   هُوَ أَشَدُّ عَرَجًا مِنْ زَيْدٍ   He is lamer than Zayd.

   هُوَ أَكْثَرُ اِجْتِهَادًا مِنْ زَيْدٍ   He is more hard-working than Zayd.

2. The words خَيْرٌ and شَرٌّ are also used for اِسْمُ التَّفْضِيْلِ.

   e.g. اَلظَّالِمُ شَرُّ النَّاسِ   The oppressor is the worst of people.

3. اِسْمُ التَّفْضِيْلِ gives رَفْعٌ to its hidden ضَمِيْرٌ.

   e.g. زَيْدٌ أَفْضَلُ مِنْ بَكْرٍ   Zayd is more virtuous than Bakr.

   The *dameer* هُوَ in أَفْضَلُ is its فَاعِلٌ.

EXERCISE

1. Translate, fill in the *i'raab* and explain the usage of اِسْمُ التَّفْضِيْلِ in the following sentences.

   i. بعض الحيوانات أقوى من الإنسان   v. النساء الفضليات

   ii. الأنبياء أفضل الناس   vi. الأنبياء أفاضل الناس

   iii. مريم فضلى النساء   vii. الرجلان الأفضلان

   iv. أولئك هم خير البرية   viii. ثوبك أشد سوادا من ثوبي

Section 4.3.6[70]
اَلْمَصْدَرُ – Infinitive/Verbal Noun

Definition: It is that noun which refers to the action indicated by the corresponding verb without any reference to time. It is the root of all derived words (مُشْتَقَّاتٌ).

Effect: It has the same effect as that of its verb i.e. it gives رَفْعٌ to the فَاعِلٌ and نَصْبٌ to the مَفْعُوْلٌ بِهِ.

e.g. رَأَيْتُ ضَرْباً الْيَوْمَ زَيْدٌ بَكْرًا   Today, I saw Zayd's beating of Bakr.

Usage:

Masdar is generally used in one of the following two ways:

- as a مُضَافٌ to its فَاعِلٌ.
  e.g. كَرِهْتُ ضَرْبَ زَيْدٍ بَكْرًا   i.e. (أَنْ يَضْرِبَ زَيْدٌ بَكْرًا)   I disliked Zayd's beating of Bakr.

- as a مُضَافٌ to its مَفْعُوْلٌ بِهِ.
  e.g. كَرِهْتُ ضَرْبَ بَكْرٍ زَيْدٌ   i.e. (أَنْ يَضْرِبَ بَكْرًا زَيْدٌ)   I disliked Zayd's beating of Bakr.

EXERCISE

1. Fill in the *i'raab* and explain the usage of the *masdar* in the following sentences.

    i. سرني قراءة رشيد القرآن   iii. إكرام العرب الضيف معروف

    ii. حبك الشيء يعمي ويصم   iv. ولله على الناس حج البيت من استطاع إليه سبيلا

---

[70] For more details, examples, and exercises, please refer to *al-Nahw al-Wadih, Thanawiyyah*, vol. 2, 52-70.

Section 4.3.7[71]
اَلْمُضَافُ

In the case of مُضَافٌ, it is assumed that one of the following prepositions (حُرُوْفُ جَرٍّ) is hidden between the مُضَافٌ and مُضَافٌ إِلَيْهِ.

- مِنْ   when the مُضَافٌ إِلَيْهِ is a part/type (جِنْسٌ) of the مُضَافٌ إِلَيْهِ.
   e.g. خَاتَمٌ فِضَّةٍ   i.e. خَاتَمٌ مِنْ فِضَّةٍ   silver ring

- فِيْ   when the مُضَافٌ إِلَيْهِ is a ظَرْفٌ.
   e.g. صَلَاةُ اللَّيْلِ   i.e. صَلَاةٌ فِي اللَّيْلِ   night prayer

- لِ   when it is neither of the above two.
   e.g. اِبْنُ زَيْدٍ   i.e. اِبْنٌ لِزَيْدٍ   Zayd's son

Section 4.3.8
اَلْاِسْمُ التَّامُّ

Definition: It is that noun, which gives the noun (تَمْيِيْزٌ) after it a *nasb*.

- A noun will be considered as تَامٌّ when it has one of the following:
   a. *tanween*.
      e.g. مَا فِي السَّمَاءِ قَدْرُ رَاحَةٍ سَحَابًا   (رَاحَةٌ)
      There is not even a palm's measure of clouds in the sky.

   b. hidden *tanween*.
      e.g. مَعِيْ أَحَدَ عَشَرَ رَجُلًا   (أَحَدَ عَشَرَ was originally أَحَدٌ وَعَشْرٌ)
      There are eleven men with me.

   c. ن of a dual noun.
      e.g. عِنْدِيْ قَفِيْزَانِ بُرًّا   (قَفِيْزَانِ)
      I have two *qafeezes*[72] of wheat.

   d. ن which resembles the ن of a sound masculine plural (جَمْعُ مُذَكَّرٍ سَالِمٍ).
      e.g. عِنْدِيْ عِشْرُوْنَ دِرْهَمًا   (عِشْرُوْنَ)
      I have twenty *dirhams*.

The اَلْاِسْمُ التَّامُّ in the above examples cannot be مُضَافٌ while having a *tanween* or having a *noon* of dual/plural, thus the noun after it gets a نَصْبٌ because of it being تَمْيِيْزٌ.

---

[71] For more details, examples, and exercises, please refer to *al-Nahw al-Wadih, Thanawiyyah*, vol. 1, 131-141.
[72] A *qafeez* is a classical Islamic measure of volume. According to the Hanafis, it is equal to 40.344 litres.

Section 4.3.9[73]

اَلْكِنَايَاتُ

Definition: It is that noun, which indicates an unspecified quantity.
- It is clarified by the noun following it.
- These are كَمْ and كَذَا.

كَمْ: can be used in two ways: as an interrogative (اِسْتِفْهَامٌ) or as an informative exclamation (خَبَرِيَّةٌ).

1. **كَمْ اَلْاِسْتِفْهَامِيَّةُ** – (how many)
   - It gives the noun (تَمْيِيزٌ) after it a نَصْبٌ.
   - The تَمْيِيزٌ is singular.
     - e.g. كَمْ كِتَابًا عِنْدَكَ How many books do you have?
   - At times, the preposition مِنْ appears before the تَمْيِيزٌ.
     - e.g. كَمْ مِنْ كِتَابٍ عِنْدَكَ How many books do you have?

2. **كَمْ اَلْخَبَرِيَّةُ** – (so many)
   - It gives the noun (تَمْيِيزٌ) after it a جَرٌّ (because of it being a مُضَافٌ إِلَيْهِ).
   - The تَمْيِيزٌ may be singular or plural.
     - e.g. كَمْ مَالٍ أَنْفَقْتَ So much of wealth you have spent!
     - e.g كَمْ أَمْوَالٍ أَنْفَقْتَ So much of wealths you have spent!
   - At times the preposition مِنْ appears before the تَمْيِيزٌ.
     - e.g. كَمْ مِنْ مَلَكٍ فِي السَّمٰوٰتِ There are so many angels in the skies/heavens!

كَذَا – (so much, such and such)
- It gives the noun (تَمْيِيزٌ) after it a *nasb*.
- The تَمْيِيزٌ is singular.
  - e.g. عِنْدِي كَذَا دِرْهَمًا I have this much *dirhams*.

EXERCISE

1. What is the difference between the following sentences.

   ii. كم كتابٍ قرأت   i. كم كتابا قرأت

---

[73] For more details, examples, and exercises, please refer to *al-Nahw al-Wadih, Thanawiyyah*, vol. 2, 170-173.

Section 4.4

اَلْحُرُوفُ الْغَيْرُ الْعَامِلَةِ – Non-Governing Particles

1. حُرُوفُ التَّنْبِيهِ – **Particles of Notification:**

   These are used to draw the attention of the listener. These are as follows:

   | أَلَا | أَمَا | هَا | meaning | Lo! / Behold! / Take heed! |

   e.g.
   - أَلَا إِنَّ نَصْرَ اللهِ قَرِيبٌ — Behold! Indeed, Allah's help is near.
   - أَمَا زَيْدٌ نَائِمٌ — Behold! Zayd is sleeping.
   - هَا أَنَا حَاضِرٌ — Lo! I am present.
   - هٰذَا — This

   <u>Note</u>: The actual اِسْمُ إِشَارَة is only ذَا, while هَا is the حَرْفُ تَنْبِيهٍ. However, in common usage the whole is referred to as اِسْمُ إِشَارَة without differentiating.

2. حُرُوفُ الْإِيجَابِ – **Particles of Affirmation:**[74]

   These are used for affirmation of a statement made earlier. These are as follows:

   نَعَمْ   بَلَى   إِيْ   أَجَلْ   جَيْرِ   إِنَّ

   نَعَمْ – (yes)
   - It is used to confirm a statement, be it positive or negative. For example,
     - If someone says أَجَاءَ زَيْدٌ؟ (Did Zayd come?), the reply will be نَعَمْ (yes) meaning جَاءَ زَيْدٌ (Zayd came.).
     - If someone says أَمَا جَاءَ زَيْدٌ؟ (Has Zayd not come?), the reply will be نَعَمْ (yes) meaning مَا جَاءَ زَيْدٌ (Zayd did not come.).

   بَلَى – (yes, why not)
   - It is used to convert a negative statement into a positive one.

     e.g. If someone says أَلَمْ يَقُمْ زَيْدٌ؟ (Did Zayd not stand up?), the reply will be بَلَى (yes, why not) meaning قَدْ قَامَ زَيْدٌ (Zayd has stood up.).

   إِيْ – (yes)
   - It is the same as نَعَمْ. However it is used with an oath (قَسَمٌ) after a question.

     e.g. If someone says أَقَامَ زَيْدٌ؟ (Did Zayd stand up?), the reply will be إِيْ وَاللهِ (yes, by Allah!) meaning قَامَ زَيْدٌ (Zayd stood up.).

---

[74] For more examples and exercises, please refer to *al-Nahw al-Wadih, Ibtida'iyyah*, vol. 3, 168-174.

(yes) – إِنَّ / جَيْرِ / أَجَلْ

- These have the same meaning as نَعَمْ.

  e.g. If someone says أَجَاءَ زَيْدٌ؟ (Did Zayd come?), the reply will be إِنَّ or جَيْرِ or أَجَلْ (yes) meaning جَاءَ زَيْدٌ (Zayd came.).

  Note: إِنَّ is very rarely used for this purpose.

3. حَرْفَا التَّفْسِيرِ – **Particles of Clarification**:

   These are used to clarify a word in a sentence. These are as follows:

   أَنْ   أَيْ   (that is)

   e.g. وَاسْئَلِ الْقَرْيَةَ أَيْ أَهْلَ الْقَرْيَةِ   And ask the town, that is, the people of the town.

   وَنَادَيْنَاهُ أَنْ يَا إِبْرَهِيمُ   And We called him, that is, O Ibraheem!

4. اَلْحُرُوفُ الْمَصْدَرِيَّةُ: These are used to give a *masdari* meaning. These are as follows:

   أَنَّ   أَنْ   مَا

   - مَا and أَنْ come before a جُمْلَةٌ فِعْلِيَّةٌ.
   - أَنَّ comes before a جُمْلَةٌ اسْمِيَّةٌ.

   e.g. (بِرُحْبِهَا) حَتَّى إِذَا ضَاقَتْ عَلَيْهِمُ الْأَرْضُ بِمَا رَحُبَتْ

   Until when the earth became straitened for them despite its vastness.

   (صِدْقُكَ) يَسُرُّنِي أَنْ تَصْدُقَ   Your truthfulness pleases me.

   (نَوْمُهُ) بَلَغَنِي أَنَّ زَيْدًا نَائِمٌ   (News of) Zayd's sleeping reached me.

   Note: أَنْ and أَنَّ are governing particles.

5. حُرُوفُ التَّحْضِيضِ – **Particles of Exhortation**:

   These are used to encourage someone to do something when they appear before فِعْلٌ مُضَارِعٌ. These are as follows:

   أَلَا   هَلَّا   لَوْلَا   لَوْمَا

   e.g. هَلَّا نُصَلِّيْ؟   Do you not pray *salah*?

   - These particles are also used to create regret and sorrow in the listener when they appear before فِعْلٌ مَاضٍ. Therefore, they are also called حُرُوفُ التَّنْدِيمِ.

   e.g. هَلَّا صَلَّيْتَ الْعَصْرَ؟   Have you not prayed 'Asr *salah*?

   e.g. وَلَوْلَا إِذْ سَمِعْتُمُوهُ قُلْتُمْ...   When you heard it, why did you not say...

6. حَرْفُ التَّوَقُّعِ – **Particle of Anticipation:**[75]

This is قَدْ. An example of its usage for تَوَقُّعٌ is as follows.

    قَدْ يَقْدُمُ الْغَائِبُ الْيَوْمَ   Probably, the absent person will return today.

- Besides تَوَقُّعٌ, قَدْ can also be used for one or more of the following. These are all more common than its usage for تَوَقُّعٌ.

  تَقْرِيبٌ: In this case, it gives فِعْلٌ مَاضٍ the meaning of near past. This usage is specific to فِعْلٌ مَاضٍ.

      e.g.   قَدْ جَاءَ زَيْدٌ   Zayd has arrived (recently).

  تَقْلِيلٌ: In this case, it gives فِعْلٌ مُضَارِعٌ the meaning of seldomness. This usage is specific to فِعْلٌ مُضَارِعٌ.

      e.g.   إِنَّ الْجَوَادَ قَدْ يَبْخَلُ   Indeed, sometimes, a generous person is miserly.

  تَحْقِيقٌ: In this case, it gives فِعْلٌ مَاضٍ or فِعْلٌ مُضَارِعٌ the meaning of certainty.

      e.g.   قَدْ جَاءَ زَيْدٌ   Certainly, Zayd came.

              قَدْ يَعْلَمُ اللهُ   Certainly, Allah knows.

- قَدْ can also be used simultaneously for more than one of the above-mentioned purposes. An example of قَدْ being simultaneously used for تَوَقُّعٌ, تَقْرِيبٌ, and تَحْقِيقٌ, is as follows:

      قَدْ قَامَتِ الصَّلَاةُ   Indeed, *salah* has been established.

Note: لَعَلَّ can also be used for تَوَقُّعٌ.

7. حَرْفَا الِاسْتِفْهَامِ – **Particles of Interrogation:**[76]

These are أ and هَلْ.

    e.g.   أَزَيْدٌ قَائِمٌ   Is Zayd standing?

            هَلْ قَامَ زَيْدٌ   Did Zayd stand up?

---

[75] This is based on *Mu'jam al-Qawa'id al-'Arabiyyah*. See *Mu'jam al-Qawa'id al-'Arabiyyah*, 338-339.
[76] For more examples, and exercises, please refer to *al-Nahw al-Wadih, Ibtida'iyyah*, vol. 3, 168-171.

8. حَرْفُ الرَّدْعِ – **Particle of Rebuke:**

This is كَلَّا, which means "Never!"

- It can be used to rebuke or reprimand.

    e.g. كَلَّا said in response to someone who says اِضْرِبْ زَيْدًا (Hit Zayd.).

- It can also be used to convey the meaning of certainty.

    e.g. كَلَّا سَوْفَ تَعْلَمُوْنَ   Indeed, soon you will know.

    Note: This is according to one translation. According to another, it is in the meaning of "never."

9. اَلتَّنْوِيْنُ: It is used for one or more of the following:

    تَمَكُّنٌ: It is that *tanween*, which shows a noun to be مُعْرَبٌ.

    e.g. زَيْدٌ

    تَنْكِيْرٌ: It is that *tanween*, which shows a noun to be نَكِرَةٌ.

    e.g. رَجُلٌ

    تَعْوِيْضٌ: It is that *tanween*, which subsitutes a مُضَافٌ إِلَيْهِ.

    e.g. يَوْمَئِذٍ   i.e. يَوْمَ إِذَا كَانَ كَذَا   the day when such and such happens

10. نُوْنُ التَّأْكِيْدِ: It is used for emphasis in مُضَارِعٌ, أَمْرٌ and نَهْيٌ. It is of two forms: ثَقِيْلَةٌ and خَفِيْفَةٌ. Both have the same meaning.

اَلثَّقِيْلَةُ (نّ)	اَلْخَفِيْفَةُ (نْ)	
لَيَضْرِبَنَّ	لَيَضْرِبَنْ	Indeed, he should hit.
أَنْصُرَنَّ	أَنْصُرَنْ	You must help.

11. حَرْفُ لَ: It can be used for the following:

    اِبْتِدَاءٌ: It appears before the مُبْتَدَأٌ, and is used for emphasis.

    e.g. لَأَنْتُمْ أَشَدُّ رَهْبَةً   Indeed, you are more feared

    جَوَابٌ: It comes in the answer to لَوْ – لَوْلَا and قَسَمٌ.

    e.g. وَلَوْلَا دَفْعُ اللهِ النَّاسَ بَعْضَهُمْ بِبَعْضٍ لَفَسَدَتِ الْأَرْضُ

    If Allah did not repel some people by means of others, the earth would be corrupted.

    وَاللهِ لَأَصُوْمَنَّ غَدًا   By Allah! I will fast tommorrow.

    زَائِدَةٌ: This is extra, and can be used for emphasis.

    e.g. إِنَّهُمْ لَيَأْكُلُوْنَ الطَّعَامَ   Indeed, they eat food.

12. اَلْحُرُوْفُ الزَّائِدَةُ – **Extra Particles:** These are not translated. However, they add beauty and emphasis to the meaning. They may also stop the effect (عَمَلٌ) of an عَامِلٌ. These are:

إِنْ   أَنْ   مَا   لَا   لَ   مِنْ   كَ   بِ   (مِنْ، كَ، بِ are governing particles – عَامِلَةٌ)

Usage:

إِنْ: It appears after مَا النَّافِيَةُ.

    e.g.   مَا إِنْ زَيْدٌ قَائِمٌ   Zayd is not standing.

أَنْ: It appears after لَمَّا.

    e.g.   فَلَمَّا أَنْ جَاءَ الْبَشِيْرُ   When the bearer of good news came.

مَا: It appears after the following:

إِذَا	e.g.	إِذَا مَا ابْتُلِيْتَ فَاصْبِرْ	When you are afflicted, be patient.
مَتَى	e.g.	مَتَى مَا تُسَافِرْ أُسَافِرْ	When you travel, I will travel.
أَيُّ	e.g.	أَيُّمَا الرَّجُلُ جَاءَكَ فَأَكْرِمْهُ	Whoever comes to you, treat him hospitably.

Here, مَا blocked the عَمَلٌ of أَيُّ.

أَيْنَ	e.g.	أَيْنَمَا تُوَلُّوا فَثَمَّ وَجْهُ اللهِ	Whichever way you turn, there is the face of Allah.
إِنْ	e.g.	فَإِمَّا يَأْتِيَنَّكُمْ مِنِّي هُدًى	Then, should some guidance come to you from Me.
حَرْفُ جَرٍّ	e.g.	فَبِمَا رَحْمَةٍ مِّنَ اللهِ لِنْتَ لَهُمْ	So, it is through mercy from Allah that you are gentle to them.

Here, مَا did not block the عَمَلٌ of حَرْفُ جَرٍّ.

لَا	e.g.	لَا أُقْسِمُ بِهَذَا الْبَلَدِ	I swear by this city.
لَ	e.g.	إِنَّهُمْ لَيَأْكُلُوْنَ الطَّعَامَ	Indeed, they eat food.
مِنْ	e.g.	هَلْ مِنْ خَالِقٍ غَيْرُ اللهِ؟	Is there a creator besides Allah?
كَ	e.g.	لَيْسَ كَمِثْلِهِ شَيْءٌ	There is nothing like Him.
بِ	e.g.	لَيْسَ زَيْدٌ بِكَاذِبٍ	Zayd is not a liar.

13. حُرُوْفُ الشَّرْطِ الَّتِيْ لَا تَجْزِمُ – Conditional Particles That Do Not Give *Jazm*:[77]

أَمَّا (however, as for, as far as...is concerned)

- It is used to explain/clarify something, which was mentioned briefly.
- ف should be used before its answer (جَوَابٌ).

  e.g. فَمِنْهُمْ شَقِيٌّ وَسَعِيْدٌ فَأَمَّا الَّذِيْنَ شَقُوْا فَفِي النَّارِ

  So, some of them will be wretched and (some) blessed. As for the wretched, they will be in the Fire.

لَوْ (if)

- It is used to negate the second sentence (جَوَابٌ) on account of the first sentence (شَرْطٌ) not being fulfilled.

  e.g. لَوْ كَانَ فِيْهِمَا آلِهَةٌ إِلَّا اللهُ لَفَسَدَتَا

  If there had been gods besides Allah in them (the heavens and the earth), they would have been corrupted.
  (There will not be corruption because there is not more than one god.)

  Note: If a و is added to لَوْ i.e. وَلَوْ, it will give the meaning of "even if/even though" and will be known as لَوْ وَصْلِيَّةٌ.

  e.g. أَوْلِمْ وَلَوْ بِشَاةٍ   Celebrate *walimah* even if it be with one (slaughtered) goat.

لَوْلَا and لَوْمَا (if such and such had not been so, ...)

- Apart from being used for تَنْدِيْمٌ and تَحْضِيْضٌ, they are also used to demonstrate that the second sentence (جَوَابٌ) cannot be attained because of the presence of the condition of the first sentence (شَرْطٌ).

  e.g. لَوْلَا زَيْدٌ لَهَلَكَ بَكْرٌ   Had it not been for Zayd, Bakr would have perished.

لَمَّا (when)

- This is a ظَرْفٌ in the meaning of حِيْنَ. It enters upon فِعْلٌ مَاضٍ.

  e.g. لَمَّا سَلَّمْتُ عَلَيْهِ رَدَّ عَلَيَّ السَّلَامَ   When I greeted him, he returned my greeting.

---

[77] For more details, examples, and exercises, please refer to *al-Nahw al-Wadih, Thanawiyyah*, vol. 2, 43-48.

14. **بَم (مَا دَام)**: It is that مَا, which has the meaning of مَا دَام (as long as).

   e.g. أَقُومُ مَا جَلَسَ الْأَمِيرُ   i.e.   أَقُومُ مَا دَامَ الْأَمِيرُ جَالِساً

   I will stand as long as the leader is sitting.

15. **حُرُوفُ الْعَطْفِ**: These have been discussed in Section 3.10.4

FINAL EXERCISE

Q: Go through the whole book and identify the various meaning and uses of the following:

أَنْ   إِنْ   لِ   أَيْ   أَيَّانَ   مَتَى   لَمَّا   مَنْ   مَا   لَا

أَنَّ   و   فَ   حَتَّى

فَالْحَمْدُ لِلَّهِ وَالصَّلَاةُ وَالسَّلَامُ عَلَى رَسُولِ اللَّهِ

APPENDIX

Studying Classical/Qur'anic Arabic

There are a number of options available for the student of sacred Islamic knowledge seeking to learn classical Arabic on his/her path to learning the *deen*. The following is a set of suggested curricula for studying Arabic language, based upon the South Asian (Indo-Paki) scholarly tradition. It is by no means the only option. To begin with, Urdu texts have been omitted. Moreover, those following other scholarly traditions (Arab, Turkish, South East Asian) may have a somewhat different set of books, although they will also find some overlap here.

The books whose names are only mentioned in English are English texts, while those whose Arabic names are also given are Arabic texts. The texts increase in difficulty and advancement downward.

General Arabic Language

Level	Texts		
Beginner to Intermediate	*Durus al-Lughah al-'Arabiyyah* vols. 1-3 (دُرُوسُ اللُّغَةِ الْعَرَبِيَّةِ) OR *Al-'Arabiyyah Bayna Yadayk* vols. 1-3 (الْعَرَبِيَّةُ بَيْنَ يَدَيْكَ)	*Arabic Tutor* vols. 1-2	*Ten Lessons*

Nahw

Level	Texts
Beginner to Intermediate	*Tasheel al-Nahw*
	Sharh Mi'at 'Amil (شَرْحُ مِائَةِ عَامِلٍ) OR
	'Awamil al-Nahw (عَوَامِلُ النَّحْوِ)
	Hidayat al-Nahw (هِدَايَةُ النَّحْوِ) OR
	Al-Ajurrumiyyah (الْآجُرُّومِيَّةُ) with commentary *al-Tuhfah al-Saniyyah* (التُّحْفَةُ السَّنِيَّةُ)
	Al-Kafiyah (الْكَافِيَةُ)
Advanced	*Sharh ibn 'Aqil* (شَرْحُ ابْنِ عَقِيلٍ) OR
	Sharh Jami (شَرْحُ الْجَامِيْ) OR
	Sharh Qatr al-Nada wa Ball al-Sada (شَرْحُ قَطْرِ النَّدَى وَبَلُّ الصَّدَى) OR
	Sharh Shudhur al-Dhahab (شَرْحُ شُذُورِ الذَّهَبِ)

The texts *al-Nahw al-Wadih li al-Madaris al-Ibtida'iyyah* vols. 1-3 (اَلنَّحْوُ الْوَاضِحُ لِلْمَدَارِسِ الْاِبْتِدَائِيَّةِ) and *al-Nahw al-Wadih li al-Madaris al-Thanawiyyah* vols. 1-3 (اَلنَّحْوُ الْوَاضِحُ لِلْمَدَارِسِ الثَّانَوِيَّةِ) belong to the intermediate to advanced level. The six volumes in general, and the three *al-Ibtida'iyyah* volumes in particular, can be used in place of, or in conjunction with *Tasheel al-Nahw*. The six could also be used in conjunction with *Hidayat al-Nahw*. Almost always, one of these texts has something that the other does not.

Sarf

Level	Texts
Beginner	*Fundamentals of Classical Arabic* vol. 1
Intermediate	*From the Treasures of Arabic Morphology*
	'Ilm al-Seeghah (عِلْمُ الصِّيْغَةِ) OR
	Shadha al-'Arf fi Fann al-Sarf (شَذَا الْعَرْفِ فِيْ فَنِّ الصَّرْفِ)

Arabic Reading/Literature

Level	Texts	
Beginner	*Al-Qira'ah al-Rashidah* vol. 1 (اَلْقِرَاءَةُ الرَّاشِدَةُ)	*Qasas al-Nabiyyin* vol. 1 (قَصَصُ النَّبِيِّيْنَ)
		Qasas al-Nabiyyin vol. 2 (قَصَصُ النَّبِيِّيْنَ)
		Qasas al-Nabiyyin vol. 3 (قَصَصُ النَّبِيِّيْنَ)
Intermediate	*Al-Qira'ah al-Rashidah* vol. 2 (اَلْقِرَاءَةُ الرَّاشِدَةُ)	*Qasas al-Nabiyyin* vol. 4 (قَصَصُ النَّبِيِّيْنَ)
	Nafhat al-'Arab (نَفْحَةُ الْعَرَبِ)	*Qasas al-Nabiyyin* vol. 5 (قَصَصُ النَّبِيِّيْنَ)
Advanced	*Mukhtarat min Adab al-'Arab* vol. 1 (مُخْتَارَاتٌ مِنْ أَدَبِ الْعَرَبِ)	*Al-Maqamat al-Haririyyah* (اَلْمَقَامَاتُ الْحَرِيْرِيَّةُ)
	Mukhtarat min Adab al-'Arab vol. 2 (مُخْتَارَاتٌ مِنْ أَدَبِ الْعَرَبِ)	

Arabic Rhetoric (*Balaghah*)

Level	Texts
Beginner	*Durus al-Balaghah* (دُرُوْسُ الْبَلَاغَةِ)
Intermediate to Advanced	*Al-Balaghah al-Wadihah* (اَلْبَلَاغَةُ الْوَاضِحَةُ)
	Talkhees al-Miftah (تَلْخِيْصُ الْمِفْتَاحِ)
	OR
	its commentary *Mukhtasar al-Ma'ani* (مُخْتَصَرُ الْمَعَانِيْ)

Suggested Curriculum

Below, we have provided a suggested curriculum based upon some of the texts given above that could be followed as part of an overall traditional Arabic & Islamic Studies curriculum. This curriculum is based on a two-semester academic year.

Year	Sem	Texts					
1	1	*Ten Lessons*		*Fundamentals* vol. 1		*Durus al-Lughah* vol. 1	
	2	*Tasheel al-Nahw* (using *Al-Nahw al-Wadih Ibtida'iyyah* & *Thanawiyyah* for reference/examples)		*Treasures of Arabic Morphology*	*Durus al-Lughah* vol. 1 (continued if not completed, followed by vol. 2)	*Arabic Tutor* vol. 1	*Qasas al-Nabiyyin* vols. 1 & 2
2	1	*Tasheel al-Nahw* (continued, if not completed) followed by selected readings & exercises from *al-Nahw al-Wadih Ibtida'iyyah* & *Thanawiyyah*		*Treasures of Arabic Morphology* (continued)	*Durus al-Lughah* vol. 2 (continued if not completed, followed by vol. 3)	*Arabic Tutor* vol. 1 (continued if not completed, followed by vol. 2)	*Qasas al-Nabiyyin* vols. 3 & 4
	2	*Hidayat al-Nahw*	*'Awaamil al-Nahw* OR *Sharh Mi'at 'Aamil*	*'Ilm al-Seeghah*		*Nafhat al-'Arab*	*Qasas al-Nabiyyin* vol. 5
3	1	*Sharh ibn 'Aqil* vol. 1		*Durus al-Balaghah*		*Mukhtarat* vol. 1	
	2			*Durus al-Balaghah* (continued, if not completed) followed by selected readings from *Talkhees al-Miftah* OR its commentary *Mukhtasar al-Ma'ani*			

BIBLIOGRAPHY

'Aamir Bashir (ed.). (2012). *Ten Lessons of Arabic*. Buffalo: Dār al-Saʿādah Publications.

'Abd al-Ghaniyy al-Daqr. (1986). *Muʿjam al-Qawaʿid al-ʿArabiyyah fi al-Nahw wa al-Tasreef* [Handbook of Arabic Grammar Rules]. Damascus: Dar al-Qalam.

'Abd al-Majid Nadvi. (n.d.). Vol. 1, *Muʿallim al-Insha'* [Composition Tutor]. Karachi: Majlis Nashriat-e-Islam.

'Abd al-Rahman al-Fawzan, Mukhtar Husayn & Muhammad 'Abd al-Khaliq. (2007). *Al-ʿArabiyyah bayna Yadayk* [Arabic Before You] *(Vols. 1-3)*. Riyadh: Al-ʿArabiyyah li al-Jameeʿ.

'Abd al-Sattar Khan. (2007). *Arabic Tutor (Vols. 1-2)* (Ebrahim Muhammad, Trans.). Camperdown, South Africa: Madrasah Inʿamiyyah.

'Abdullah ibn 'Aqil. (1980). *Sharh ibn ʿAqil ʿala Alfiyyat ibn Malik* [Ibn ʿAqil's Commentary on *The One-thousand Verse Poem* of Ibn Malik] *(Vols. 1-4)*. Cairo: Dar al-Turath.

Abul Hasan 'Ali al-Nadwi. (n.d.). *Al-Qira'ah al-Rashidah* [The Rightly Guided Reading] *(Vols. 1-2)*. Karachi: Majlis Nashriat-e-Islam.

Abul Hasan 'Ali al-Nadwi. (n.d.). *Mukhtarat min Adab al-ʿArab* [Selections from the Literature of the Arabs] *(Vols. 1-2)*. Karachi: Majlis Nashriat-e-Islam.

Abul Hasan 'Ali al-Nadwi. (n.d.). *Qasas al-Nabiyyin* [Stories of the Prophets] *(Vols. 1-5)*. Karachi: Majlis Nashriat-e-Islam.

'Ali al-Jaarim & Mustafa Ameen. (n.d.). *Al-Balaghah al-Wadihah* [Clear Rhetoric]. Cairo: Dar al-Maʿarif.

'Ali al-Jaarim & Mustafa Ameen. (n.d.). *Al-Nahw al-Wadih li al-Madaris al-Ibtida'iyyah* [Clear Grammar for Elementary Schools], *(Vols. 1-3)*. Cairo: Dar al-Maʿarif.

'Ali al-Jaarim & Mustafa Ameen. (n.d.). *Al-Nahw al-Wadih li al-Madaris al-Thanawiyyah* [Clear Grammar for Secondary Schools], *(Vols. 1-3)*. Cairo: Dar al-Maʿarif.

Al-Andalusi, ibn Hayyan. (2008). *Hidayat al-Nahw* [Guide to Grammar]. Karachi: Maktabat al-Bushra.

Al-Ansari, Abdullah ibn Hisham. (1994). *Sharh Qatr al-Nada wa Ball al-Sada* [Commentary on *The Drops of Dew and the Moisture of Thirst*], with notes by Muhammad Muhy al-Din 'Abd al-Hamid. Beirut: al-Maktabah al-ʿAsariyyah.

Al-Ansari, Abdullah ibn Hisham. (1990). *Sharh Shudhur al-Dhahab* [Commentary on *The Scattered Particles of Gold*]. Beirut: Maktabat Lubnan.

Al-Hamlawi, Ahmad ibn Muhammad. (2005). Muhammad ibn 'Abd al-Muʿti (ed.). *Shadha al-ʿArf fi Fann al-Sarf* [Strong Fragrance Regarding the Science of Morphology]. Riyadh: Dar al-Kayan.

Al-Hariri, Muhammad al-Qasim ibn 'Ali. (n.d.). *Al-Maqamat al-Haririyyah* [The Assemblies of al-Hariri]. Lahore: Maktabah Rahmaniyyah.

Al-Jurjani, 'Abd al-Qahir. (n.d.). *Sharh Mi'at 'Amil* [Commentary of Hundred Governing Words]. Karachi: Qadimi Kutubkhana.

Al-Qazwini, Muhammad ibn 'Abd al-Rahman. (2010). *Talkhees al-Miftah* [Summary of *The Key*]. Karachi: Maktabat al-Bushra.

Al-Taftazani, Mas'ood ibn 'Umar. (2010). *Mukhtasar al-Ma'ani* [Summary of Rhetoric]. Karachi: Maktabat al-Bushra.

Charthawali, Mawlana Mushtaq Ahmad. (n.d.). *'Ilm al-Nahw* [Science of Grammar]. Karachi: Altaf & Sons.

Charthawali, Mawlana Mushtaq Ahmad. (2010). *'Awamil al-Nahw* [Governing Words of Grammar]. Karachi: Maktabat al-Bushra.

Dockrat, Mawlana Hasan. (2003). *Tawdeeh al-Nahw: A Simplified Arabic Grammar*. Azaadville, South Africa: Madrasah Arabiah Islamia.

Ebrahim Muhammad. (2006). *From the Treasures of Arabic Morphology*. Camperdown, South Africa: Madrasah In'amiyyah.

Husain Abdul Sattar. (2002). Vol. 1, *Fundamentals of Classical Arabic*. Chicago: Faqir Publications.

Ibn al-Hajib. (2008). *Al-Kafiyah* [The Sufficient]. Karachi: Maktabat al-Bushra.

Jami, 'Abd al-Rahman. (2011). *Sharh al-Mulla al-Jami 'ala al-Kafiyah* [The Commentary of Mulla Jami on *The Sufficient*]. Karachi: Maktabat al-Bushra.

Lane, E. W. (1968). Book I, Parts 4-6, *An Arabic-English Lexicon*. Beirut: Librairie du Liban.

Muhammad Diyab, Sultan Muhammad, et. al. (2009). *Durus al-Balaghah* [Lessons of Rhetoric]. Karachi: Maktabat al-Bushra.

Muhammad 'Inayat Ahmad. (n.d.). *'Ilm al-Seeghah* [Science of Forms]. (Wali Khan al-Muzaffar, Trans.). Karachi: al-Maktabah al-Faruqiyyah.

Muhammad I'zaz 'Ali. (2010). *Nafhat al-'Arab* [Fragrance of the Arabs]. Karachi: Maktabat al-Bushra.

Muhammad Muhy al-Din 'Abd al-Hamid. (1989). *Al-Tuhfah al-Saniyyah bi Sharh Muqaddamat al-Ajurrumiyyah* [The Sublime Gift of Commentary on the *Ajurrumi Prolegomena*]. Cairo: Maktabat al-Sunnah

V. 'Abd al-Rahim. (2009). *Durus al-Lughah al-'Arabiyyah* [Lessons of Arabic Language], *(Vols. 1-3)*. Chennai: Islamic Foundation.

Made in United States
North Haven, CT
26 October 2023